GW00686339

The pocket guide to
Birds of Prey
of Britain and Europe

Peter Hayman & Rob Hume

MITCHELL BEAZLEY

The Pocket Guide to the Birds
of Prey of Britain and Europe
By Peter Hayman and Rob Hume

First published in Great Britain in 2006
by Mitchell Beazley, an imprint of
Octopus Publishing Group Limited,
2–4 Heron Quays, London E14 4JP.

Copyright © Octopus Publishing Group
Limited 2006
Text copyright © Rob Hume 2006

A CIP catalogue record for this book
is available from the British Library.

ISBN 1 84533 184 2

The author and publishers will be
grateful for any information that will
assist them in keeping future editions up
to date. Although all reasonable care has
been taken in the preparation of this
book, neither the author nor the
publishers can accept liability for any
consequences arising from the
information contained herein, or from the
use thereof.

Commissioning Editor: Vivien Antwi/
Jon Asbury Executive Art Editor: Yasia
Williams-Leedham Managing Editor:
Juanne Branquinho Editor: John
Woodward Design: Kenny Grant
Picture Research: Jenny Faithfull
Production: Gary Hayes

Typeset in Garamond and Gill Sans
Printed and bound by Toppan Printing
Company, China

Photographic credits: 12/17 Aquila/Juan Martin Simon; 26/27 Windrush Photos/Roger
Tidman; 29 Windrush Photos/David Tipling; 30 Aquila; 31 Windrush Photos/Colin
Carver; 38/41 Windrush Photos/Richard Brooks; 42 Windrush Photos/Roger Tidman; 43
Aquila/R T Mills; 52/53 Windrush Photos/Arthur Morris; 55 Windrush Photos/Frederic
Desmette; 56 Windrush Photos/George McCarthy; 57 Windrush Photo/D Mason, 64/65
Windrush Photos/Peter Cairns; 67 Windrush Photos/E A Janes; 68 Windrush
Photos/Peter Cairns; 69 Windrush Photos/Roger Powell; 82/83 Aquila/Juan Martin
Simon; 84/85 Windrush Photos/Peter Cairns; 86 Aquila/Juan Martin Simon; 87
Windrush Photos/Roger Powell; 104/107 Windrush Photos/Richard Brooks; 108
Aquila/Juan Martin Simon; 109 Windrush Photos/John Lawton Roberts; 130/131
Windrush Photos/David Tipling; 132 Windrush Photos/Pentti Johansson; 134 Aquila/G
F Date; 135 Aquila/N W Harwood; 162/163 Windrush Photos/Richard Brooks; 165
Aquila/Conrad Greaves; 166 Windrush Photos/John Davies; 167 Aquila/H Kinloch

Honey-buzzards

Secretive and solitary in summer,
honey-buzzards migrate south in large
and spectacular flocks each autumn

Contents

Greater spotted eagles
These magnificent eagles breed in
eastern Europe, but occur in the
Mediterranean region in winter

Introduction
Rob Hume

Birds of prey come in many shapes and sizes, and some are dramatic, charismatic birds. In the opinion of many people, few species in Europe match the lammergeier for sheer spectacle, and many others would rate the peregrine high on any list of perfectly adapted hunters. While there are those who feel that birds of prey attract more than their fair share of attention, most people experience a thrill of excitement when they see one, and want to know what it is.

Becoming proficient at identifying birds of prey takes time and patience. It involves watching them as often as possible, which is a hugely enjoyable exercise. It also requires good references, so that we can be sure of what we are looking at. Peter Hayman's carefully measured and beautifully executed paintings, based on years of experience in the field and detailed research in the museum, provide the ideal reference material for beginner and expert alike.

HABITATS

Symbols show the main habitats in which each bird can be found: these are shorthand guides, not an exhaustive list.

MOUNTAINS AND TUNDRA

WOODLAND AND FOREST

FOOTHILLS, UPLANDS, AND MOORS

HEATHS AND ROUGH GRASSLAND

CLIFFS, CRAGS, AND QUARRIES

LAKES AND MARSHES

FARMLAND

URBAN AND SUBURBAN AREAS

20–30cm 8–12in

SCALE INDICATORS
Each bird is shown to scale compared with a woodpigeon in flight (grey at top right). The size shown is the average length from tail to beak. If the bird is smaller than 60cm (24in) long, it is shown at a scale of 1:67; if larger, at a scale of 1:133.

DISTRIBUTION MAPS
Birds of prey breed in areas marked **red**; they spend the winter, or are seen on migration, in areas marked **blue**; they can be seen all year in areas marked **purple**. A few species, including some of the owls, are more or less nomadic and wander rather irregularly outside the breeding season.

Most of us see a few birds of prey regularly and hope to see others just a few times each year. Inevitably, some will 'get away', leaving a question mark in the notebook. This is the case with all birds, but birds of prey are especially likely to appear in difficult circumstances. Because of their size and conspicuousness, many species can be seen at great distances against bright skies. At such times their behaviour often provides the best clue to their identity: a kestrel, for example, is usually betrayed by its hovering hunting style, not its plumage.

This book also includes the owls: nocturnal counterparts, for the most part, of birds of prey but not in any way related to them. Owls are elusive, but if anything this increases their appeal. It also includes shrikes: these are not birds of prey in any technical sense, but they do prey on other birds, small mammals, reptiles, and insects, and can be as exciting to watch as any hawk or falcon.

Peregrine
A thickset, bullet-headed
bird at rest, the peregrine is
one of the world's most
dramatic aerial hunters

What is a bird of prey?
Raptorial birds

Birds of prey around the world vary from some of the biggest of all flying birds to miniature falcons that are smaller than starlings. In Europe they range from huge eagles to the relatively tiny male merlin and sparrowhawk, no larger than a mistle thrush.

They are equally variable in terms of their shape, lifestyle, habitat, distribution, and numbers. They feed on anything from small insects to large birds and mammals the size of a roe deer, as well as fish, reptiles and all kinds of refuse, offal, and dead meat (carrion). Not all kill their food: vultures feed on animals that are already dead.

Despite this broad spectrum of form and behaviour, they are all linked by common features. All have hooked bills; falcons have a 'tooth' on the upper mandible and use this to kill prey with a strong bite to the neck, but most birds of prey kill with their strong feet,

Black-shouldered kite
Some species have more than one English name, and this one is also known as the black-winged kite; the commonest alternatives are given in brackets in this book

crushing their prey and piercing it with their powerful claws or talons. While vultures have blunt claws and honey-buzzards have short, strong toes that are ideal for digging out wasps' nests, most species have long, curved, strong, sharp claws, perfect for dealing with prey. Ospreys have spiky scales on their toes to grasp slippery, muscular fish.

Birds of prey have large, more or less forward-facing eyes to give excellent binocular vision. This characteristic is even more obvious in their nocturnal counterparts, the owls. Owls also have excellent hearing and some species have asymmetrical ears, enabling them to pinpoint the exact position of the slightest sound in three dimensions. They can locate a mouse in the dark, or even under snow, by using their hearing rather than their sight. Owls also have other special features, such as a fringe of soft barbules along the outer edge of each flight feather, to give them a wonderfully silent flight. Sometimes, surprise is the best form of attack.

The shrikes are songbirds, but have evolved several features associated with birds of prey, especially their slightly hooked beaks and strong, sharp claws. They are small, but fierce and highly predatory birds.

Imperial eagle
There is debate about certain forms: are they species, or races? Imperial and Spanish imperial eagles are treated as two species in this book

Tawny owl
Several species come in more than one form, either well marked (such as booted eagles), or more subtle, as in the case of grey or brown tawny owls

How to identify a bird of prey
Time and patience

A great eagle expert, Leslie Brown, once said that he could not understand why people found birds of prey difficult to identify, as they were six feet across and flew high in the sky, unlike tiny, secretive warblers. That is true of some species, and a few are so distinctive that confusion seems hardly possible: the black-shouldered kite is one of these. Others, however, are undoubtedly a challenge, and some 'species pairs' are extremely difficult to distinguish: female hen harriers and Montagu's harriers, for instance, or female kestrels and lesser kestrels.

Much depends on circumstances. For example, the black kite is very rare in Britain and many UK reports fail to be accepted. This can be a tricky species, and too many records fail to exclude the possibility of a marsh harrier or some other confusion species. Yet in its more usual context, such as in Spain, it is easy to identify a black kite flying away at long range, with the naked eye, even from a fast-moving car. Such recognition often relies heavily on shapes and flight actions: perched birds are more rarely seen and can be remarkably hard to identify with any certainty.

Experience is the essential element: a book such as this cannot provide that. Instead, you must watch birds of prey as often and for as long as possible, which is hardly a hardship. Taking notes and making sketches, however rough, will help plant the details in your memory and enable you to check doubtful identifications.

Short-toed eagle
Basic elements remain the same, but variations in colour, pattern, and shape can confuse the issue

Booted eagle

Look at shapes and patterns: this eagle has an unusual array of markings, including white shoulder spots, a pale diagonal band across the inner wing and a broad pale U-shape above the tail; other species are less well marked, and shape and action are more help

PALE WING COVERT BAND

PALE INNER PRIMARY PATCH

FINGERED PRIMARY TIPS

Honey-buzzard

The wing pattern can be almost matched by a buzzard, but the tail bands are unique and the set of the wings, held flat or drooped, and with an S-shaped trailing edge, is characteristic

The parts of a bird of prey
Feather tracts and structure

Birds of prey have the same basic feather tracts as other birds: the wings, for example, have several rows of coverts (small at the front, becoming larger further back), and larger, stronger flight feathers (secondaries on the inner wing, or 'arm', primaries on the outer wing, or 'hand'). These can be used to describe patterns: the osprey shown opposite has white lesser and median coverts, black-barred greater coverts (giving a dark midwing band), and dark primary coverts (creating the obvious 'wrist patch'); the secondaries are boldly barred, the primaries are extensively tipped with black, and the tail has several narrow bands. These feather tracts are invaluable aids to precise description, and since there are only a few terms to learn it is worth giving them some time and attention.

The skeletal structure of the wing includes a short humerus and long 'forearm' (radius and ulna) before the 'wrist' or carpal joint, which is frequently a prominent feature in flight. It is often important to note whether the wing is held upwards, flat, drooped, or angled at the carpal joint; whether the primary tips are spread apart ('fingered') or taper neatly to a point. In many circumstances

Marsh harrier
This female shows a clear-cut head pattern (pale cap, dark mask, pale throat) and pale shoulders (lesser wing coverts) as well as long, yellow legs and a yellow cere at the base of the bill

FEATHERED THIGHS

TARSUS (LOWER LEG)

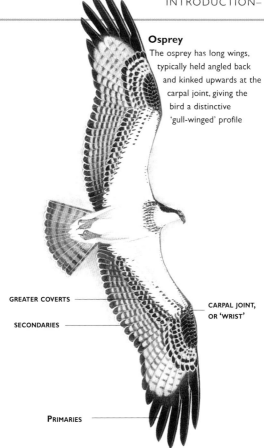

Osprey

The osprey has long wings, typically held angled back and kinked upwards at the carpal joint, giving the bird a distinctive 'gull-winged' profile

GREATER COVERTS

SECONDARIES

CARPAL JOINT, OR 'WRIST'

PRIMARIES

these structural features and shapes are more useful than colours and patterns when trying to identify flying birds of prey, although they are rather less helpful in the case of most owls.

The bill of a bird of prey is hooked, and it has a bare, fleshy patch at the base called the cere. This is usually yellow on an adult bird of prey, but bluish or dull on a juvenile. The eyes also have bare, fleshy skin around them, typically also yellow (but sometimes red) on adults. Some species have yellow eyes, some black, others reddish; owls have dark or penetrating yellow eyes.

The legs and feet may be bare, as on hawks and falcons, although long thigh feathers may cloak the upper leg. Other species such as many eagles and owls have feathered or 'booted' legs.

Vultures

Vultures can seem gruesome at close range, but they are magnificent in the air. They are highly developed birds, adapted for feeding on the remains of dead animals; most species take little or no live food. No European vulture relies on a sharp sense of smell, as do some American species: they all find their food by sight.

Habitat
Open vistas

Since they rely on sight to find food on the ground, European vultures fly mostly over open spaces such as fields, pastures and wild grasslands, from lowlands to high Alpine peaks. They spread out widely over vast areas, soaring high up, but each remaining in view of a few of its fellows. If one bird sees food and descends, others notice and quickly move over to join it. They avoid dense undergrowth and forests with closed canopies. Nevertheless, Egyptian vultures can often be seen over wooded hillsides, searching the smaller gaps between trees, and as black vultures nest in trees they cannot live in areas totally devoid of woodland.

It is not unusual to see three species together, as their habitat preferences overlap considerably. Lammergeiers, for example, prefer high valleys with sheer cliffs, but they also search open landscapes of all kinds and frequently cross forested slopes to reach their feeding areas. A cave or deep ledge sheltered by a broad overhang is essential

for roosting and nesting. Griffon vultures need cliffs with wide ledges for breeding and roosting throughout the year.

An essential component of any vulture's habitat is open air, with suitable updraughts that help to keep them aloft with minimal use of energy. They are heavy birds and direct, active flight with deep beats of their broad wings is very demanding. Vultures must exploit rising air currents: either 'bubbles' of warm air (thermals) rising from bare slopes warmed by the sun, or updraughts caused by strong winds sweeping over hillsides that keep them aloft even in cold conditions.

They are unable to make long sea crossings, as there are no rising air currents and soaring is impossible, so like other birds of prey, storks, and pelicans, migrant vultures heading to and from Africa concentrate over the narrowest sea crossings at each end of the Mediterranean, especially at Gibraltar and the Bosphorus.

Rocky vantage point
Griffon vultures spend much of their time on ledges of rock, usually with views across wide open plains, valleys, or gorges. Sunbathing helps them keep their feathers in good condition.

Feeding
Irregular meals

Griffon vulture: gruesome table manners
A typical Old World vulture, the griffon is able to detect food at long range from high in the air. It prefers fresh meat such as sheep, goats, or chamois that have been dead for just a day or two.

Large vultures may go for several days without food, but will gorge themselves with meat whenever they get the opportunity. In Europe, they rely largely on dead deer, sheep, cattle, chamois, and goats in upland areas. As animal carcasses have become scarcer, quite large numbers in parts of Spain, France, Greece, Bulgaria, and elsewhere are sustained by supplementary feeding with offal from abattoirs. Griffon vultures have recently been known to attack live sheep in Spain, a phenomenon that is thought to be an unexpected result of the large numbers now found in relatively small areas.

The lammergeier is a specialist at eating bones, which it breaks open by dropping them onto rocks from a height. The Egyptian vulture has a slender bill and narrow head that enable it to penetrate into small cavities within a carcass, but it is unable to rip open tough hides. The toughest of these are tackled by the strongest species with the biggest bill: the black vulture. Between them, the four species are neatly adapted to their various roles.

Breeding
Variations on a theme

Lammergeiers nest in isolated pairs in large cavities in sheer cliffs, often beneath overhangs that give shelter and make their nests inaccessible to people and other land-based predators. Griffon and Egyptian vultures, however, are colonial, and the two species frequently nest together on long cliff ledges with an open outlook that allows them to sweep up to and away from the nest without obstruction. An overhang often gives some shelter from spring rain and summer sun. Large areas splashed with white droppings betray a vulture colony or roosting site from afar.

Black vultures differ in that they build large, bulky nests of thick sticks in the flat tops of trees. They sometimes select quite small cork oaks, especially in the Spanish *dehesas*, or plains with scattered trees and orchards.

Reproduction is a long, slow business: vultures may not breed until five or six years old, and griffon and black vultures lay just one egg, the others one or two. Incubation lasts up to 55 days and the young do not fly until they are 100 or 120 days old.

Black vulture: tree-nesting exception
While the other vulture species in Europe nest on bare ledges, black vultures breed in large tree nests built of sticks, often in otherwise rather open plains.

Griffon Vulture
Gyps fulvus

95–110cm (37–43in)

DISTRIBUTION
Mostly resident in Spain, Portugal, S France, Balkans; some move south in winter; most common in Spain

◄ Adult
Looks pale on ground, unlike black vulture; head bristly, pale, with bulbous yellowish bill; blunt rear end with very short tail; bare grey legs; often moves with two-footed leap or shuffling gallop, wings half spread in aggression near food

Flight shapes ►
Wingtip broad, but separated feathers twist upwards; as bird turns, so the wings change from broad and round to narrow and pointed and back again, because of uptilted, warped shapes; inner wing has marked upward and rearward bulge

▼ Underside
Pale wing coverts with variable paler bars; flight feathers dark brown, blacker at distance; juvenile richly coloured, neater, with toothed trailing edge

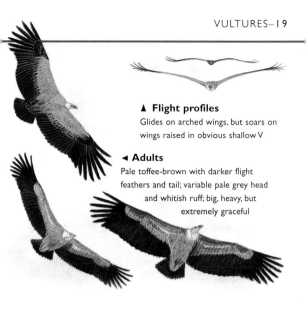

▲ Flight profiles
Glides on arched wings, but soars on wings raised in obvious shallow V

◄ Adults
Pale toffee-brown with darker flight feathers and tail; variable pale grey head and whitish ruff; big, heavy, but extremely graceful

IDENTIFICATION A massive brown bird, the size of a large dog but looks bigger on open ground, with small, greyish head, rounded, pale bill; perches upright. In flight has huge, broad, fingered wings with bulging trailing edge; shape changes as it circles from 'pointed wing' to 'round wing', but it always has a very short tail and tiny head and holds its wings in a slight V when it soars. It looks tawny/toffee brown with darker flight feathers, which become worn and battered with age before being replaced with neater, darker, fresh ones. Juveniles lack such variation in age of feathers and look more uniform in colour and neatness. In cold air, has deep, ponderous wingbeats; in hot air, soars endlessly with frequent wide, slow circling in impressive display of aerial skill.

HABITAT Nests on rock ledges in gorges or high on isolated cliffs; feeds on open ground from high, barren, rock-strewn peaks to river valleys, tips and low-lying farmland.

BEHAVIOUR Griffons are always fascinating; at the colony, they often fly in close formation in twos, threes, or fours, in chevrons or line astern, swinging in to the ledges with dangling legs and feet, which look remarkably long and heavy. On cold mornings they gather where the wind sweeps up over a slope and can be watched very low down, even over villages, but on hot days they wait for rising air later on in the morning and then sail away from the colony at great heights, to disperse over vast areas in search of food.

Black (Monk) Vulture
Aegypius monachus

145–160cm (57–63in)

DISTRIBUTION
Very local in central
and SW Spain,
Balkans, mostly NE
Greece, Bulgaria;
rare and irregular
wanderer outside
breeding range

▲ From below
Broad, rather parallel-sided
wings with primaries often
angled back, less shapely than
griffon; very dark forewing

▲ Adult
Extremely dark in fresh plumage,
fades browner; always darker, less
tawny than griffon, with wing coverts
darkest; juvenile has saw-tooth
rear edge to wings; short, slightly
wedge-shaped tail; pale feet often
conspicuous

◄ Soaring
Irregular paler band on
midwing appears as
feathers fade with age

▲ Diving away
Upswept wingtips give pointed
effect from certain angles

◄ Soaring
Looks huge, broad-winged,
with flat, straight-edged,
door-like shape

◀ In flight
Griffon (top) soars
on raised wings;
black (lower) on flat
or bowed wings

IDENTIFICATION A huge black-brown bird with a short, wedge-shaped tail, the black vulture is less shapely, more rectangular and even more like a 'flying door' than the griffon. On the ground, shows its pale head with a dark face patch well at long range; dark ruff is hard to see, but gives a different impression from the pale-necked griffon. In flight, tends to look darker on the wing coverts than on the greyer

Head pattern ▲
Powerful head and
bill with striking
pattern visible at
very long range

flight feathers, the reverse of the griffon; it has flat or drooped wings, giving a more menacing look than the more graceful griffon. It often looks rather ragged and heavily worn in flight.

HABITAT Forages over open ground, farmland of all kinds, clearings in hillside forests, and high peaks. It needs trees for nesting, so is usually close to woodland of some sort.

BEHAVIOUR Often sits around for long periods, even on flat, open ground, but usually seen in flight. Rises mid-morning on warm days over wooded hills and peaks, not usually so high in barren mountains as the griffon. Mostly scarcer than the griffon and often seen in twos or threes when there may be 50 or more griffons in the sky, but in parts of Spain it is commoner. The dominant bird at a carcass, with the most powerful bill, it can usually see off griffons.

On ground ▶
Big, angular, wide-shouldered; pale pinkish
and bluish head and bill base contrast with
dark face patch, bill tip and ruff, giving
more menacing look than griffon; bill
deeper than on other vultures

Lammergeier (Bearded Vulture)
Gypaetus barbatus

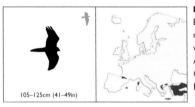

105–125cm (41–49in)

DISTRIBUTION
Extremely local, most in Pyrenees, very rare in the Alps (reintroduced), Crete and SE Europe

Soaring ►
Stunning shape with long, tapered, graceful wings and wedge- or diamond-shaped tail, longest on slender-winged males; small 'beard' visible in close view

IMMATURE   ADULT

IDENTIFICATION

Combines huge size with extreme grace: the lammergeier can sail slowly backwards and forwards along a cliff face or circle in the open sky for minutes on end without a hint of a wingbeat, or give one or two very deep, powerful beats. Whitish head is often eye-catching at great distances; the long tail is the next feature to be sure of. Adults look very dark but may 'shine' charcoal- or silver-grey above in sunlight; good light also reveals warm rusty-orange below. Immatures are dark and pale grey, browner in a close view. Usually looks smaller than griffon, despite greater overall length, but females can be massive.

HABITAT High peaks, barren slopes, and rocky plateaux; deep, rocky gorges and sheer cliff faces; also lower down over forested and open slopes and farmland.

BEHAVIOUR Often spends long periods motionless in a cave or on a ledge, when hard to detect, but then suddenly 'appears' against the sky, or as a dark shape sailing along the face of the cliff. Lammergeiers cover huge areas in gliding flight, or circle high over peaks, but may be seen in short views crossing valleys or disappearing into gorges. They can be watched, usually at long range, dropping bones onto rocky slopes to break them open.

▲ Adult
Basically dark grey, with pale head and orange-buff to cream underside; male more slender, female broader-winged

JUVENILE

▼ Juvenile
All dark at first; older immatures have dark hood and wings, pale grey body, often pale inner primaries

Flight ▶
Glides with head turned down, looking for food; soars on flat or drooped wings, circling to great heights for long periods; direct flight also easy, sailing with 'everlasting glides' and only occasional very deep, slow, powerful wingbeats

UNDERSIDE

ADULT

▼ Mature birds
Old birds have white heads, undersides discoloured by oxides, often rich orange; upperside brownish-grey, shining pale in sun

ADULT

ADULT

Egyptian Vulture
Neophron percnopterus

55–65cm (22–26in)

DISTRIBUTION
Mostly scarce, local; summer visitor to Iberia, S France, S Italy, SE Europe, some larger islands

From above ▲
Whitish with darker flight feathers, blackest on wingtip; wedge-shaped white tail; yellow face and ochre-yellow head

IDENTIFICATION Adult has white stork pattern of black flight feathers and white body, wing coverts, and tail. On the ground it may look grubby, but the narrow yellow face is obvious; in flight it usually looks immaculate white or glows pink-buff in bright sun against blue sky. Immatures are less often seen (they mostly remain in Africa until adult); they are all dark, eagle-like, but the narrow head and wedge-shaped tail help; older immatures have a paler band across the underwing.

HABITAT Wooded and more open hillsides with rocks and cliffs. Nests and roosts on ledges or in cavities, often in loose association with colonies of griffon vultures. Feeds on ground on hillsides, refuse tips, and farmland, with other vultures and kites.

BEHAVIOUR Often seen with other vultures, which make it look small – although in reality it is a big, impressive bird – the Egyptian vulture is equally adept at soaring and gliding, with a great mastery of the air. Tends to be seen in twos and threes in company with tens or dozens of griffons, but can be found in small groups on its own, or with kites, crows, and ravens around refuse tips. Where it is not persecuted it quite often flies low over people at quite close range, giving superb views, but does not usually allow such a close approach on the ground, taking to the air with a series of small leaps.

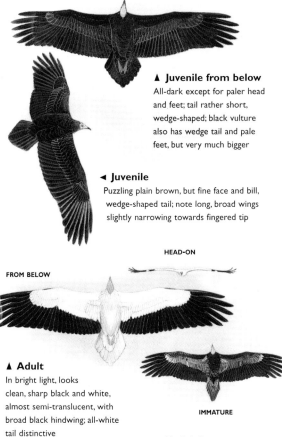

▲ Juvenile from below
All-dark except for paler head
and feet; tail rather short,
wedge-shaped; black vulture
also has wedge tail and pale
feet, but very much bigger

◄ Juvenile
Puzzling plain brown, but fine face and bill,
wedge-shaped tail; note long, broad wings
slightly narrowing towards fingered tip

HEAD-ON

FROM BELOW

▲ Adult
In bright light, looks
clean, sharp black and white,
almost semi-translucent, with
broad black hindwing; all-white
tail distinctive

IMMATURE

▼ Adult
Basically white, with blackish
across wing (whiter areas on
wing wear away to reveal more
black); yellow face

▼ Juvenile
Plain dark brown with thin bill,
bare pink face, spiky crown,
heavily-feathered thighs but
bare feet, long tail; quite
long, thick neck
characteristic

Kites

Two European kites, the red and black, are very similar in appearance and behaviour, although the red kite is largely resident while the black is a summer visitor, wintering in Africa. The third, the black-shouldered or black-winged kite, is markedly different, although several very similar species are found in other continents.

Habitat
Simple requirements

Black and red kites need trees to nest in, and open ground over which to forage. They mostly live quite comfortably close to people, visiting village rubbish heaps, larger tips, landfill sites near towns, farms, and even gardens in some areas. Some reintroduced red kites in southern England are even fed in gardens. The once-familiar sight of kites over town and city streets, however, is becoming less frequent as the waste food and refuse of all kinds that they exploit is cleared away more efficiently. The black kite and the closely similar yellow-billed kite that occupy large areas of the tropics are declining in many regions as hygiene improves. In Europe, the black kite shows signs of spreading north as the climate warms, but intensive farming and ever-increasing coastal development threaten it in the south, removing its habitat and feeding opportunities.

Red kites like mixed landscapes with open pastures and wooded hillsides. In Britain they were almost wiped out by persecution in the early 20th century and became restricted to parts of central Wales. The habitat – varied countryside with bogs, moorland, heaths, small pastures, and plentiful trees – was ideal but their subsequent recovery was severely restricted by the cold wet weather in spring, occurring at a critical time for their young chicks. They have now been reintroduced into similar habitats in England and Scotland, in both upland and lowland areas.

Black kites are able to exploit drier areas, even semi-deserts, and are generally commoner around Mediterranean coastal districts, but intensive agriculture reduces opportunities for them and they are now surprisingly scarce over large areas. On the other hand, they tend to be more closely associated with waterside habitats than red kites, and they take a good deal of food from the surface and shorelines of lakes and rivers when they can.

Both species nest in trees and require some woodland, or at least mature shelterbelts and copses, in otherwise open areas where they can hunt easily. They also roost in trees rather than on open ledges. In mountainous areas, such as the Pyrenees, red kites (but rarely black kites) forage right up over the highest peaks, sometimes being seen accompanying groups of vultures, but they are not normally birds of barren rocky ground, cliffs, or gorges.

Black-shouldered kite
The European population is a small extension of a much wider range across Africa. This handsome bird has close relatives in America and Australasia but is quite unlike any other European bird of prey.

Black-shouldered kites are widespread in Africa but very restricted in Europe, living in warm, wild areas with cork oaks, olive groves, and rough grassland in parts of Spain and Portugal. They often occur near water and frequently hunt over marshland, but they are not birds of dense forest, nor of exposed mountainous regions. Like other kites, they rely on their excellent eyesight to find food, and need relatively open ground over which they can hunt, ideally with a scattering of tall perches – either human artefacts such as pylons and poles, or large trees with dead branches – from which they can see prey on the ground.

Feeding
Opportunistic foraging

Anyone who has experienced a black kite stealing food from a picnic can confirm that these seemingly lightweight, elegant birds pack a surprising punch and are able to dive in at great speed. They are also agile enough to snatch a meal from a plate or a sandwich from your hand. Their apparently light, airy flight masks considerable power and excellent close-quarters manoeuvrability.

Black and more often red kites can kill small to medium birds and mammals up to the size of a rabbit in a sudden stoop, using their strong legs and feet. Some red kites take many young birds, such as crows and gulls, from their nests in summer; some individual kites seem to specialize in this activity. More often, however, these two species survive on scraps and carrion. They take offal and rubbish of all kinds wherever they can find it, and dead animals ranging from the sheep and deer that die on open hillsides in winter to rabbits and birds killed by traffic on roads.

Black-shouldered kites take a lot of small birds such as corn buntings, many voles and mice, lizards, and large insects such as beetles. They hunt by watching from posts or treetops, or hovering over open ground and dropping onto their prey.

Sharing a meal
A dead sheep or cow in southern Europe will attract vultures that can open the carcass to feed; red kites may arrive too, but cannot feed until the vultures have cut through the thick hide.

Breeding
Tree nesters

Recycled nest material
Red kites weave all kinds of material, including wool, scraps of
paper, and even plastic bags, into the sticks and small branches
that form the foundation of their large nests.

All three species make big nests of sticks, lined with finer material.
Each nest is surprisingly well-hidden in the leafy canopy of a tree.
Red and black kites use all kinds of rubbish in the structure,
including paper, plastic, and discarded cloth, and add a pad of sheep's
wool to the lining. Black kites add fresh greenery; this may help to
reduce the risk of disease and parasites. If a nest has been used
successfully, it may be refurbished and used again the following year.

Red and black kites lay two or three eggs, while black-
shouldered kites lay three or four. The eggs are incubated for some
26–28 days. Young black-shouldered kites fly at 35–40 days, and
black kites at about 42 days, but red kites may not fly before 48–50
or even 60 days old, partly depending on the availability of food. Red
kites begin to breed when they are two years old.

Red Kite
Milvus milvus

61–72cm (24–28in)

DISTRIBUTION
Widespread in
S and C Europe
and Britain; summer
migrant in north
of range

▲ From beneath
Pale head; long, pale,
notched tail; black wingtips
and large white patch
under outer wing; black
kite never so contrasted

RED KITE

BLACK KITE

▲ Comparison
Red kite brighter than
black kite, with much
whiter wing patch
underneath and paler tail;
both have angled wing,
unlike buzzard

ADULT

▲ Head-on
Black (top) and red
circle on bowed or
angled wings

◄ Upperside
Broad, diffuse, pale band
across forewing; pale head;
tail pale to rich rusty-red;
small, downcurved head

In flight ►
A beautiful, elegant bird, with slow, flexible wingbeats and frequent twists of long, notched tail; typically floats more lightly than buzzard in direct flight, and circles on flatter wings

IDENTIFICATION   A large, brightly patterned bird with relaxed, elegant 'elastic' wingbeats in direct flight, its wings slightly angled. Soars with wings bowed, not raised in a V. The tail is pale from beneath but rusty-red above; forked when closed, but notched or triangular with sharp outer corners when spread. Pale bands across the upperwings and white patches beneath are distinctive. Loud, long, ringing squeal or wavering call.

HABITAT Typically mixed habitats, with open fields, heath and scattered woodland, often close to rivers; also high peaks and moors.

BEHAVIOUR Usually in twos or threes, sometimes in much larger gatherings where they are fed, as in central Wales; often occurs with black kites in parts of Europe. Flies steadily with regular, easy wingbeats and few glides, or circles for long periods, often to a great height, sometimes with vultures high overhead, looking minute in comparison. Often seen on the ground, in Britain frequently feeding on worms after rain in fields, usually with buzzards, or feeding on a dead rabbit in a field or on a roadside.

On ground ▼
Long, slim, diagonal stance; big feathered thighs; wing coverts pale with sharp black centres

JUVENILE

ADULT

Black Kite
Milvus migrans

48–58cm (19–23in)

DISTRIBUTION
Widespread but
generally scarce
summer visitor in
SW, S, SE, C and
NE Europe; rare
wanderer elsewhere

IDENTIFICATION Generally very like a dull red kite with a less deeply-forked tail; also like a female marsh harrier, but with rather more obvious pale patches under the wing and, more usefully, a strong, pale, diagonal band on each upperwing and a slight bow to

▲ Gliding away
Notice bowed or arched wings,
tail held low and often twisted
or tilted sideways

the wings in a glide. Does not soar with its wings in a V, as do both the buzzard and the marsh harrier. Juveniles quite rusty below but darker than a red kite overall, with a much duller tail; underwing patch is not so white. Although sometimes confusing, it is usually an easy bird to identify given a reasonable view. Loud squealing calls, much like red kite.

HABITAT Often in river valleys and riverside woods, where there are fields, orchards, villages with tips, and farmland nearby. In some areas occurs over towns, but declining in urban and suburban habitats generally as they have become much cleaner, with little food. May be spreading slowly north with a warming climate.

BEHAVIOUR More associated with water than the red kite, often dipping down to take food from the surface using its feet, but the two species are often seen together and sometimes not so easy to separate as might be expected, although a good view will soon remove any doubt. It is often seen in pairs, or sailing along on its own, but can be found in much bigger concentrations; in Southern Europe it usually occurs in larger numbers than the red kite. It is not infrequently seen perched on a tall telegraph pole or pylon, very upright, like a slim dark buzzard. Black kites often associate with Egyptian vultures and crows in the vicinity of open tips.

▲ On ground
Slender, long-tailed;
darker, plainer than most
buzzards and red kite; thighs
dark rufous, not bright

MODOLORE

RED KITE

Juvenile ▶
Pale feather edges, even
whitish spangling on upperside
on well-marked birds; paler
rufous below approaches that of
red kite; often hint of dark mask

▲ From below
European birds typically
dark and plain with faint
pale wing patch; tail
triangular, scarcely notched

From above ▶
Obvious pale diagonal band across
inner wing; tail notched when
closed; rather drab, but dull
brown, not really black

Black-shouldered Kite
Elanus caeruleus

31–35cm (12–14in)

DISTRIBUTION
Extremely local in
Portugal and NW
and W Spain

▲ Adults
Handsome pale grey, white, and black;
large, pale head; elegant, easy flight but
looks rather wide-winged and short-
tailed; bold black shoulder patches
obvious from above

Juvenile ►
White areas soiled brownish and buff,
upperside barred brown and white

From below ►
Thickset, with broad wings; mostly clear white with black wingtips

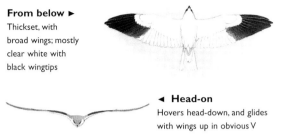

◄ Head-on
Hovers head-down, and glides with wings up in obvious V

IDENTIFICATION A gentle-looking, round-headed bird, the black-shouldered (or black-winged) kite usually looks very pale, grey above and whiter below. It is very upright and broad-headed when perched. From above, the inner wing has a black shoulder patch; from below, the black is on the wingtip. The shoulder patch shows well when the bird is perched. Its frequent hovering, like a large, floppy kestrel, is obvious, as is the usual flight with glides on quite markedly V-shaped wings. When gathering speed it may look a little more falcon-like, with its wings angled back.

HABITAT Open countryside with marshy ground near rivers, and among lines of trees near open farmland.

BEHAVIOUR Typically perches on top of a tree, or at the end of a dead branch, making it easy to see, or flies out over open ground in search of food. When hunting it frequently rises a little then hovers in one spot, head bent down to look intently at the ground, then moves on to hover again, or dives head first into the grass.

From below ▼
Adult crisply white, juvenile duller; male smaller than broad-winged female at all ages; black wingtip recalls male hen harrier

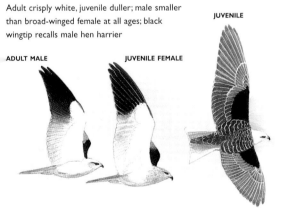

JUVENILE

ADULT MALE

JUVENILE FEMALE

Harriers

Pallid and Montagu's harriers are summer migrants from Africa. Hen harriers move in winter to more southerly and low-lying regions. Marsh harriers from north and east Europe migrate to Africa or Mediterranean areas, while those that breed in the south-west and south are resident or wander randomly in winter.

Habitat
Narrow requirements

Harriers are birds of rather open ground, with low, rolling hills and moors rather than peaks, crags, or cliffs. In suitable places, such as the reedy river channels that are followed by hunting marsh harriers, they may be seen close to towns and villages or over farmland, which is the chief habitat of Montagu's harrier. Hen harriers in particular also live in wild, remote moorland areas in summer, where they favour slopes covered with dense growths of heather, and damp, rushy valley bottoms.

Marsh harriers rely on reeds or bullrushes (redmace) for nesting and roosting, although they wander widely over nearby farmland to feed. So while they are widespread, they are very localized everywhere in Europe. Montagu's harriers have a wider range of habitats, including heaths, reedy marshes, and cultivated farmland with cereal crops, but much of the farmland has now been rendered unsuitable

for breeding harriers by intensive cultivation and mechanized operations in spring and summer. In areas such as the UK, most Montagu's harriers' nests now require special protection, or at least cooperation from landowners, if they are to succeed.

Harriers are not woodland birds, and they avoid trees for the most part. Despite this, marsh harriers perch freely in isolated trees and bushes growing in or close to reedbeds, and hen harriers nest within extensive young pine plantations, before the growing trees create a dense canopy. Marsh harriers often stand on open ground but others more frequently use low posts, stumps, and rocks as perches.

Hen harriers in plantations

Young conifer plantations are ideal for hen harriers for a few years, but quickly become too tall and dense. The harriers are then excluded from vast afforested areas.

Feeding
Low-level hunters

Marsh harrier
The largest harrier, this powerful hunter takes prey up to the size of coots and ducks if it can catch them. More typically it eats smaller prey caught at the edges of reedy pools.

The typical hunting flight of a harrier is a low, concentrated patrol, the bird looking intently at the ground with its head bent down. It looks slow, but hen harriers, for example, can quickly cover a lot of ground. In likely places, such as clumps of heather, tussocky rushes, and at the edges of reedbeds, the birds may hover and float almost motionless. Open ground, such as close-cropped, grassy pasture in winter, is covered at speed; in such places the harriers use their greater momentum to chase small birds that they scare into flight.

Harriers have unusually long legs: the length of the bare lower leg is obvious but the upper leg, usually hidden by the body feathers, also extends quite considerably. This give them a long 'reach' that helps them catch prey in tall grass, cereal crops or reeds.

Marsh harriers take larger prey such as small ducks, moorhens, coots and their young from water, as well as voles, rats, young rabbits, and other small mammals. The other species prefer small rodents, reptiles, and smaller birds such as pipits and finches, or the young of larger species taken before they can fly in summer.

Breeding
Ground nesters

In spring, harriers display high over their nesting areas with energetic, acrobatic manoeuvres and noisy, repetitive calls. While the female incubates the eggs, the male catches prey and brings it back, calling the female off the nest to transfer the food in a dramatic 'food pass' in mid-air. As with several other birds of prey, females moult some of their flight feathers while they are more or less immobile in the incubation stage. If there is a good food supply male harriers may mate with two or more females, and feed both them and their broods.

Their nests are pads of vegetation on the ground, well concealed among heather, grass, or crops, or in reeds. Up to eight unmarked eggs may be laid, hatching after 29–38 days. The female incubates as soon as the first egg is laid, so the earliest eggs hatch first and the chicks are markedly different in size. In good years most or all will be reared, but if food is short the smaller ones lose out to their older siblings and soon die. The surviving young fly after about six weeks.

Harriers are extremely vulnerable to human persecution at this stage, as they are bold and aggressive in defence of their nests, diving at the heads of intruders who venture too close.

Dominant chicks

Like some owls, harriers hatch their eggs over several days. The early chicks are much bigger than the later ones and monopolize the food if there is insufficient to go round.

Marsh Harrier
Circus aeruginosus

43–55cm (18–22in)

DISTRIBUTION
Widespread but
everywhere local;
mostly a summer
migrant, but
resident in parts
of S Europe

IDENTIFICATION A buzzard-sized, broad-winged, heavy harrier. Older males are strongly patterned, while females and young males are chocolate brown with variable creamy-yellow marks on the head and shoulders. The brown back, grey tail and grey wing patches of a male are much more distinct than on the brownish-backed immature male Montagu's or hen harriers. A soaring female could be mistaken for dark buzzard or black kite, but lacks their pale underwing patches and diagonal pale bands across the upperwing; harriers also typically soar with their wings in a V.

HABITAT Relies on reedy swamps and fens, but also hunts over open land of all kinds, especially pastures and dunes.

BEHAVIOUR A typical harrier, keeping mostly low to the ground except in spring displays, flying steadily head-to-wind but quite fast when turning to glide downwind to a new feeding area, or in a brief chase after prey. Often perches on dead trees or bush tops in marshes, but nests deep within the reeds.

◄ Males
Often breed in sub-adult
plumage with grey areas
mixed with brown;
older birds
become purer
grey on wings
and tail

Juvenile male ▲
Juvenile has narrow pale feather
fringes; basically dark brown with
pale head; male more slender-
winged than female

Mature male ▼
Most richly-coloured harrier,
sandy-buff on head,
rufous below

Adult female ▲
Dark chocolate brown with variable
cream-buff or yellow-buff patches
on head and shoulder

JUVENILE

Flight ▲ ►
Soars with wings well forward;
glides with wings raised in V

MALE

FEMALE

◄ ▼ In flight
Short head, long tail usually closed, but
fanned in tight manoeuvres; wingtips
slightly swept back

OLDER MALE

IMMATURE
MALE

FEMALE

◄ From below
Compare female with
black kite: does not have
arched wings, and pale head
pattern well defined; male three-toned

Hen Harrier
Circus cyaneus

45–55cm (18–22in)

DISTRIBUTION
Widespread but
local; summer
migrant in N and E
Europe, winter
visitor or resident
in S and W

▼ **Adult male**
Pale dove-grey and white; plain
head with yellow eye,
small bill

▲ **Adult female**
Rich brown, streaked
below; head pattern weak,
but hint of pale-edged dark
cheek; long, banded tail

▲ **Juvenile female**
Long, barred wings, white rump;
underside more rufous than
adult's; male similar but slimmer,
with narrower wings

▲ **Adult female**
Earth-brown and cream with
bold white rump; broad dark
bars on hindwing

From below ►
Adult (left) and juvenile (right) males, slimmer than female but blunter-winged than Montagu's; adult's white rump and dark trailing edge distinctive

IDENTIFICATION Male pale grey, female and immature brown, all with white rump. Male's black wingtips, dark trailing edge to wing and white rump are a unique combination. Females are broader-winged than Montagu's or pallid harrier; young males are smaller, more similar, but still have shorter, blunter wingtips than Montagu's. Typical harrier flight with wings in V in glides, but likely to be confused only with other harriers: white rump separates it from buzzards and hawks. Loud *wek-wek-wek-wek* in spring.

HABITAT Open moorland, marshy ground, damp pastures, fields of crops in the lowlands; reedbeds and bogs, especially in the winter.

BEHAVIOUR Hen harriers hunt over wide open areas with short vegetation, or where there are clearings in thickets and young plantations. In spring, males soar high up and perform dramatic displays, with lapwing-like twists and deep undulations.

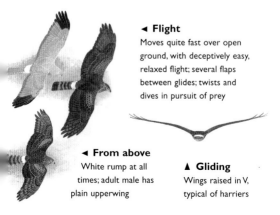

◄ **Flight**
Moves quite fast over open ground, with deceptively easy, relaxed flight; several flaps between glides; twists and dives in pursuit of prey

◄ **From above**
White rump at all times; adult male has plain upperwing

▲ **Gliding**
Wings raised in V, typical of harriers

Montagu's Harrier
Circus pygargus

40–50cm (16–20in)

DISTRIBUTION
Summer visitor to most of Europe, but extremely local; commonest in Iberia, rare in UK

IDENTIFICATION The three harrier species with grey and black males and brown females with white rumps and barred tails ('ringtails') can be difficult to distinguish, but their range and the time of year help. A male Montagu's has little or no white on the rump, a black midwing bar, a barred underwing and streaked flanks. Females and immatures are like hen harriers, but more lightly built; their longer, swept back, more tapered wingtips are often the best clue; also a stronger head pattern, with clearer whitish area around the eye and dark ear patch. Their shape and light, buoyant flight are the most useful features; also Montagu's is not found in Europe in winter, unlike the hen harrier. Loud, repetitive, fast chattering calls.

HABITAT Open landscapes with wide, undulating cereal fields, reedbeds, extensive grassy heaths, and downs.

▲ **Adult male**
Slender shape, narrow black upperwing bar; forewing often darker than hindwing

BEHAVIOUR A typical harrier of cultivated land and extensive marshes, overlapping in habitat with both hen and marsh harriers. It hunts in the same way as the hen harrier but with a slightly more elegant, relaxed or flexible wing action, carefully quartering huge areas of ground. It often perches on posts, rocks, or lumps of earth, but rarely in trees. As with other harriers, males often soar high over the breeding territory and drift across the sky, sometimes calling, or perform more energetic spring display flights, with rapid dives and steep climbs with twisting, rolling manoeuvres at the top.

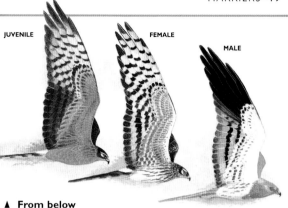

JUVENILE   FEMALE   MALE

▲ From below

Juvenile clear rufous; female boldly streaked; male barred on wing and streaked on flanks, unlike hen and pallid harrier; wingtips long, narrow, tapered, giving slightly more whippy flight action

Female ►

Like hen harrier but rump patch often smaller, wings narrower; inner wing more barred than hen or pallid, but can be difficult to distinguish

◄ Tails from beneath

Female and juvenile (lower) have three or four dark bands; compare with pallid

Juvenile ▼

Like young hen harrier but richer, plainer rufous below; stronger head pattern with white around eye and dark cheek crescent

▲ Male

Slender when perched; very long wings and tail; very thin, spindly legs and small, weak bill; dark wingbar distinctive if visible

Pallid Harrier

Circus macrourus

40–50cm 16–20in)

DISTRIBUTION
Rare summer
visitor in extreme
E Europe; elsewhere
a vagrant; winters in
Africa

Adult female ►
Very like Montagu's;
dark bars of primaries
curve around primary
covert patch leaving
clear buff band
(broken by dark bars
on Montagu's)

▼ Adult male
Like hen harrier, but black
wingtip patch narrower,
more wedge-shaped;
breast whiter

▼ Tail pattern
From below, shows
narrow outer bars
and two broad, dark
central bands

IMMATURE MALE

JUVENILE

FEMALE

▲ Juvenile
Like Montagu's, but dark hindneck,
paler collar, and dark cheek crescent
below white eye patch

IDENTIFICATION A typical harrier with grey adult male, brown female with barred (or 'ringed') tail and white rump. Mature male best identified by white underside and narrow wedge of black on wingtip, but immature male developing these features is more difficult. Female is like Montagu's, but stronger head pattern includes black eye line, white cheeks and throat, black crescent on ear coverts, and stronger pale collar. Collar more pronounced on young birds, which also have a dark hindneck shawl. Pallid has a darker axillary (wingpit) patch with finer pale spotting, a generally darker inner wing beneath, and plainer, less distinctly barred hindwing above, but differences from both Montagu's and stockier, broader-winged hen harrier are subtle.

Male ▲
Upperside of wingtip has narrow wedge of black

HABITAT Mainly dry grassland, avoiding trees, woodland and marshy places, but migrants can appear almost anywhere.

BEHAVIOUR Typical harrier, using more arid terrain than Montagu's but otherwise similar, hunting small prey on the ground. Prey is eaten on the ground, apart from small insects which may be swallowed in flight.

Male ►
Old males are the palest harriers, with body plumage of almost gull-like whiteness

Juvenile ▼
Strongest head pattern: bold dark cheek and dark hindneck are distinctive

Hawks

The true, or bird-hunting hawks share general characteristics of shape, colour, and structure, including a marked disparity in size between males and females. Their different sizes allow them to exploit different prey species, so they can occupy smaller territories without competing with each other for food.

Habitat
Woodland hunters

All the bird-eating hawks require woodland to some degree, and are unable to nest, rest, roost, or feed in wholly open landscapes. Goshawks, the largest species, are found mostly in extensive forest, either lowland or upland, deciduous or coniferous, with big trees, but also in areas with fragmented woodland and many forest clearings or cultivated patches. In winter, especially, they may also hunt over more open areas, but they are remarkably elusive and for most of the time keep well inside the woodland canopy.

Sparrowhawks can use much smaller patches of woodland or clumps of trees, and regularly visit town parks, suburban gardens, and other places with plenty of small birds. They can be seen, for example, over saltmarshes and tidelines where finch and pipit flocks concentrate in winter. They often hunt over farmland, flying low and using hedgerows both as cover – a surprise attack is best – and as likely places to find their prey. Sparrowhawks are especially characteristic of mature deciduous woods and large areas of coniferous forest or old plantations. Many of these plantations lie adjacent to upland moors, and sparrowhawks will exploit these too, hunting pipits and other birds on the moorland edge. When a hawk catches a bird it may eat it on the ground in a sheltered area or, if the site is too exposed, carry it off to a favoured 'plucking post' within a nearby patch of woodland.

Sparrowhawks become remarkably bold at times, seeming almost oblivious to human presence when they are in pursuit of small birds and occasionally giving wonderful close-up views. This sometimes leads to their downfall, as they are frequent victims of collisions with garden objects such as fences, wires, and washing lines, as if they are quite reckless in their single-minded pursuit of prey. In the heat of the chase they may occasionally enter buildings, and even open vehicles.

Levant sparrowhawks are more restricted in their European (and world) range. They are migrants, moving to and from Africa in large flocks that cross the narrows between the eastern Mediterranean and the Black Sea. In summer they prefer warm river valleys and forested slopes, especially with alders, oaks, and chestnuts. They are then solitary, as are the other species all year round.

Their woodland habitat has helped shape the hawks into efficient predators of enclosed spaces. They have broad wings, with a large surface area, and rather long tails that can be reduced to narrow 'rudders' for steering in tight spaces, or spread into a broad, rounded vanes for extra lift. These adaptations give the birds excellent control within the confines of a wood – or garden – as well as the ability to soar well high in the open air. They have a fast, direct flight, using a series of rapid, deep wingbeats between short, flat glides; this gives a useful first clue to the identity of a flying hawk.

Sparrowhawks can live in small territories in mixed woodland, and become quite common. Goshawks need much bigger territories, and they are very aggressive to other birds of prey, often killing smaller hawks and falcons to claim 'exclusive' use of an area of forest. While all hawks can be elusive, keeping within the cover of a wood, they fly high over their nesting territories in spring, when they are most easily located.

Deep forest hunter

A goshawk usually keeps well below the woodland canopy and is difficult to locate except in spring, when it displays above the trees and may sit on an exposed perch.

Feeding
Surprise attacks

Although all these hawks are essentially bird eaters, the goshawk – which is a much bigger bird than the others – also eats small mammals up to the size of squirrels and rabbits. Sparrowhawks eat almost any small or medium-sized bird they can catch: the smaller males concentrate on small finches, sparrows, tits, and similar-sized species, while the larger females take more thrushes, starlings, collared doves, and woodpigeons.

All hawks feed almost exclusively on live prey. Most is caught in a sudden surprise dash, rarely in a prolonged chase in the open; sometimes a hawk can be seen engaged in a frenzied attack on birds inside a bush or hedge. A sparrowhawk may also sit in wait inside a hedge until a group of small birds passes by, unaware of its presence.

Plucking post
Sparrowhawks have favoured perches to which they take their prey, plucking the body feathers and eating the meat. They may feed on large birds over several sessions.

Breeding
Tree nesters

A large brood
Sparrowhawks can rear five or six young if food is plentiful, in a rather flat nest of sticks with little lining, built close to the main trunk of a tall tree.

Hawks build their nests in tall trees, usually close to the main trunk on a horizontal side branch. A sparrowhawk's nest may be mistaken for a squirrel's drey, but it is a more coherent structure of thin sticks and twigs, with a flattish top. A goshawk's nest is a larger version of the same thing, made of thicker sticks, sometimes built up into an enormous pile almost surrounding the trunk, more than a metre deep and well over a metre across.

Usually four to six unmarked eggs are laid and incubated for 33–35 days (35–38 by the larger goshawk). Young goshawks fly after six or seven weeks, sparrowhawks within 24–30 days. Hawks may be quite vocal at the nest, and some goshawks are determined and intimidating in their defence of nests, diving at intruders. Despite being so secretive and difficult to locate, goshawks choose their nest sites very early in the year when few people are about in the woods. By the time they have young, the nest may prove to be surprisingly close to a well-used track or even a picnic site.

Sparrowhawk
Accipiter nisus

29–34cm (11–13in)

DISTRIBUTION
Almost all of
Europe except the
treeless north;
summer visitor in
far north and east

IDENTIFICATION A small, long- and narrow-tailed hawk; male with swept wings recalls merlin, soaring bird may suggest kestrel. Displaying female with slow, deep wingbeats suggests male goshawk. Sparrowhawk more angular than goshawk, with sharper tail corners, a smaller, shorter head, less bulging wings, weaker head pattern, slimmer legs and feet, and smaller bill. Immatures barred, not streaked. High, squealing chatter.

HABITAT Woodland of all kinds, adjacent areas of farmland, heath, marsh, and moor; often in suburban parks and gardens.

BEHAVIOUR Often seen soaring or flying high overhead (warning calls of starling are a good clue), but hunts low down, taking prey by surprise: often inconspicuous until a sudden brief, close view. In spring, soars over woodland territories, displaying with slow wingbeats, undulations, and fast headlong dives.

Adult male ▼
Bluish-grey above, barred rufous below, rufous cheeks; spotted white on back during moult

JUVENILE

Female ▼
Much bigger than male, whiter below with dull bars, stronger white stripe over eye

FEMALE

JUVENILE

Flight ►►

From below, has broad wings with slight S-shaped rear edge and long, narrow tail; flying away or diving, wingtips can look pointed, like kestrel; flight typically a series of flaps between short, flat glides

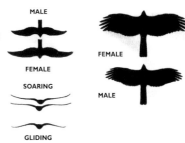

MALE

FEMALE

SOARING

GLIDING

FEMALE

MALE

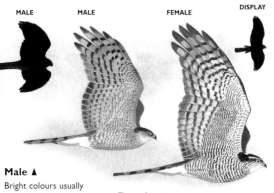

MALE MALE FEMALE DISPLAY

Male ▲

Bright colours usually look dark at distance; fast action, with snappy wingbeats, quick climbs, twists and turns; dives into enclosed spaces to surprise prey

Female ▲

Slightly slower, heavier than male but still sharp-actioned, fast-flying bird with flap-and-glide flight; underside looks dull pale grey in good light

Juvenile female ▼

Browner than adult; all females bigger, heavier, broader-winged than males; smaller, lighter, squarer-tailed, with less bulging wing than goshawk

▲ Juvenile male

Bright, rusty, with rufous bars above, brown bars on orange-buff below

Goshawk
Accipiter gentilis

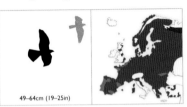

49–64cm (19–25in)

DISTRIBUTION
Almost all of
Europe except
treeless areas, rare
or scarce in many
areas; wanders
widely in winter

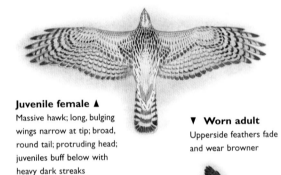

Juvenile female ▲
Massive hawk; long, bulging
wings narrow at tip; broad,
round tail; protruding head;
juveniles buff below with
heavy dark streaks

▼ Worn adult
Upperside feathers fade
and wear browner

Fresh adult ►
Upperside feathers blue-
grey when new but
become browner over
several months

Juvenile ►
Rich buff; underside
streaked, unlike any
sparrowhawk;
long, barred tail;
thick yellow legs
on all goshawks

◄ Northern birds
Adults (barred) and
juveniles (streaked, left) in
N Europe often very pale,
with 'frosted' effect

IDENTIFICATION Large hawk, males bigger than sparrowhawk, with rounder and broader tail, often darker cap, and stronger pale stripe over eye. Females much bigger, buzzard-sized, longer-winged, with broad, rounded tail, bulging hindwing, and much more protruding head than sparrowhawk. In dive with swept wings, can recall peregrine or gyrfalcon. Loud, woodpecker-like calls.

HABITAT Woodland of all kinds, both extensive, unbroken tracts and mixed woodland scattered through farmland or beside moors.

BEHAVIOUR Elusive despite its size, soaring over territories early in year, otherwise mostly close to or beneath the forest canopy. May perch conspicuously high on a tree, often dropping out of sight immediately it moves; occasionally circles up and moves away in a long glide to a different patch of forest.

Flight shapes ▲
Females not always sparrowhawk-like, males more so

FEMALE

MALE

MALE SPARROW-HAWK

FEMALE SPARROW-HAWK

Compare ▲
Note shapes and sizes, compared to scale with sparrowhawk; compare with nearby crows or other birds if possible

Male from below ▼
Dense bars give mid-grey effect; dark cheeks and cap; white under tail striking, but can be so on sparrowhawk

Female ▶
Big head obvious in side view; bold white patch beneath tail; heavy flight with slow wingbeats

Levant Sparrowhawk
Accipiter brevipes

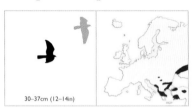

30–37cm (12–14in)

DISTRIBUTION
Local summer visitor to Balkans and further east; almost unknown outside regular range

Males ▼
Small, neat; adult (left) barred rusty-pink, juvenile (right) boldly spotted with black

Female ▼
Barred rusty below; plain head; dark central line on throat

IDENTIFICATION A small hawk, very like a sparrowhawk and not easily separated in a brief view, but has more falcon-like wings with tapered tips. The male is pinker below, its underwing white with a small black wingtip (the most distinctive feature); its cheeks are plain grey without pinkish-orange. The female also has a plainer head than a sparrowhawk: on both sexes, the dark eye and plain cheeks give a more bland expression. The female's paler underwing with a dark tip is distinctive but much less striking than on the male; unbarred central tail feathers may help distinguish it from a sparrowhawk in a close view. The juvenile has unique dark tear-drop spots on white underparts. It is easily identified when travelling in large flocks on migration. Shrill *keee-wik* calls.

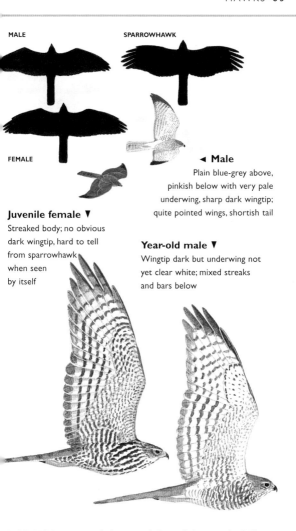

MALE

SPARROWHAWK

FEMALE

◄ Male
Plain blue-grey above,
pinkish below with very pale
underwing, sharp dark wingtip;
quite pointed wings, shortish tail

Juvenile female ▼
Streaked body; no obvious
dark wingtip, hard to tell
from sparrowhawk
when seen
by itself

Year-old male ▼
Wingtip dark but underwing not
yet clear white; mixed streaks
and bars below

HABITAT Low, wooded areas and forested slopes in foothills. It migrates over narrow sea crossings.

BEHAVIOUR A secretive hawk, less dashing than the sparrowhawk, usually hunting quite low and catching much of its prey on the ground. It is generally seen singly in breeding areas, where it is an elusive bird, not easy to see at all well. On migration, however, it soars more freely in thermals and travels in large, dense, often swirling flocks, quite unlike the sparrowhawk or goshawk.

Buzzards

This large family of medium-large birds of prey, found almost worldwide, is typified by the common buzzard in Europe. Not so large as many eagles, nor so dramatic as some of the falcons, buzzards are nevertheless impressive and often beautiful birds, marvellous in the air, able to circle high in the sky for hours on end.

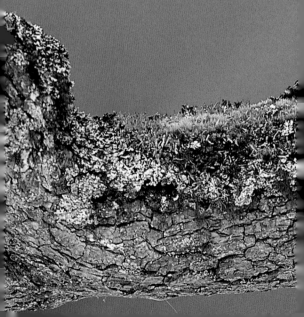

Habitat
Generalists and specialists

Common buzzards require some trees, ideally in mixed landscapes with woods or copses, heaths, moors, and farmland – especially grassy pastures. Crags often form part of a buzzard's territory but are not essential. The birds hunt over high, open moors in summer, but also in softer country, especially along river valleys, and over marshy ground in winter. They frequently perch on low posts, and often stand on open ground or on low mounds or rocks. With increased protection and a cleaner environment, the buzzard has become the commonest bird of prey in Britain and has spread back into many eastern and southern areas from which it had long been absent.

Rough-legged buzzards are found all around the Arctic. In Europe they breed in northern Scandinavia, but are more widely, if sparsely distributed in winter. They breed high up on cold, barren mountains and in the northern tundra, in wholly treeless areas with low-growing vegetation and enormous vistas. In winter rough-legged buzzards frequently occur close to the coast or in low-lying, marshy areas, where they may perch on isolated trees.

Long-legged buzzards occupy barren, rocky areas and the edges of woodland, so long as there are cliffs and some open grassland nearby, often in semi-arid areas. They are scarce in Europe, being restricted to the south-east where they are summer migrants.

The rough-legged buzzard and many common buzzards breed far enough north to make a move south or south-west in winter essential, but many buzzards are resident in west, central, and southern Europe. The steppe buzzard is a long-distance migrant, moving in large flocks to and from Africa.

All species, but especially the common and long-legged buzzards, make great use of open skies above their territories, soaring on thermals which provide lift over warm ground. They exploit these to circle high up in territorial displays – which often simply involve being visible – or to carry them over large areas in search of food.

Honey-buzzards are not closely related; they are forest birds and generally much more elusive. They are migrants and move in large flocks over the narrowest sea crossings. The osprey is wholly unrelated to buzzards; it is also a migrant, arriving each spring from Africa, but is widespread throughout the world.

Prominent perch

Common buzzards make use of perches such as fence posts and telegraph poles, as well as trees, where they are easy to see and identify. This buzzard is typical: some are much paler.

Feeding
Mixed fare

Common buzzards have powerful legs and feet, with long, sharp, arched claws, and they can catch and kill mammals up to the size of a rabbit or small hare. They also catch many small or medium-sized birds, including young crows taken from nests before they can fly. Buzzards also eat a lot of dead meat, such as rabbits killed by traffic on roads, and feed on dead animals such as sheep on moorland in winter. Yet much of the food of a buzzard is small animals, including mice, voles, beetles, and even earthworms taken after rain.

In summer rough-legged buzzards specialize in catching lemmings and voles, plus occasional rabbits, and they frequently seize young birds on the ground. Rough-legged buzzards hover to locate food much more regularly than most buzzards, although they all can and do hover well at times. Long-legged buzzards also eat a range of small mammals, from voles to ground squirrels, as well as small reptiles and large insects, plus a small number of birds.

The unrelated honey-buzzard eats adult bees and wasps and their grubs, and wax excavated from bees' nests. It perches inside a wood and watches the insects' flight lines to locate their nests, which it then digs out with its feet.

Ospreys specialize in fish, which they seize in their feet after an initial hover and spectacular headlong dive into the water.

Rough-legged buzzard on dead roe deer
Buzzards are not specialists in eating dead animals, as are the vultures, but they will not pass up the chance of a free meal.

Breeding
Tree and crag nests

Cliff nester
Rough-legged buzzards breed in areas where there are no trees, and nest on a cliff ledges or even on low rocks on near-level ground if no other options are available.

Buzzards are territorial, but many of their social interactions involve small groups, especially early in the year. Their displays involve much circling high over the breeding territory, a pair often rolling together and touching feet, with loud, ringing calls. This helps to reinforce the pair bond each year. Soaring also acts as a simple visual display to neighbouring pairs, emphasizing to others that the territory is occupied, and occasionally whole groups of buzzards gather to fly together, for reasons that are not entirely understood.

Nests are made of thick sticks and twigs with a softer lining, typically in the crown of a tree in the case of a common buzzard, usually on a crag and rarely in a tree for the other two species. Honey-buzzards nest inconspicuously in trees; they have a dramatic 'butterfly flight' display, clapping their wings together above their backs. Ospreys make big stick nests that are often visible from afar.

Three or four eggs are usual for the buzzards; they are pale buff or whitish with copious rusty-brown marks. The eggs hatch after about four weeks and the young fly when around seven weeks old.

Common Buzzard
Buteo buteo

46–58cm (18–23in)

Adult ▼
Classic medium-dark type: brown
above, narrow bars on tail, streaks
on sides of chest and flanks

**JUVENILE (LEFT) AND
ADULT TAIL FEATHERS**

IDENTIFICATION A large, broad-winged, round-tailed, brown bird of prey, usually with an obvious wing pattern beneath, including a dark wrist patch and a whitish area towards the wingtip. Very variable; eastern birds (moving west in winter) often much paler, even almost wholly creamy-buff. Often hovers, but usually seen soaring in wide circles on raised wings, or perched in upright but rather squat pose with dark and pale U-shapes on chest obvious. Loud, ringing *pee-yaa* call, more mewing at long range.

HABITAT Mixed woodland, farmland, river valleys, moorland, crags and cliffs. Usually breeds in rather low places, in or on the edge of woodland, but may hunt over higher, more open moors.

BEHAVIOUR A typical buzzard, using prominent perches on trees and tall poles, soaring frequently in wide, slightly wavering circles. Flies between perches or over longer distances in a steady, purposeful flight, with a slightly jerky wing action, less 'elastic' than rough-legged or honey-buzzard. Often seen on the ground, where it eats worms and insects, catches moles, or feeds on dead animals.

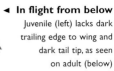

◄ In flight from below
Juvenile (left) lacks dark
trailing edge to wing and
dark tail tip, as seen
on adult (below)

Flight shapes
Stocky, medium-large bird with
broad, round wings, broad tail
rounded when spread; soars with
wings held up in distinct V-shape
and pushed well forwards

Soaring ▲
Pairs often display in tight circles;
male and female very alike, little
difference in size or shape

From below ▲
Typical dark wingtips and wrist
patches with pale area between;
juveniles plainer than adults; some
much whiter birds occur

◄ Variation
Pale birds (left)
are common in
east of range and
NW Europe in winter,
but bulk of breeding
birds in W and S Europe
look darker (right)

Steppe Buzzard
Buteo (buteo) vulpinus

DISTRIBUTION
NE and E Europe, replacing common buzzard; summer visitor, migrating south-east in autumn

46–50cm (18–20in)

JUVENILE

DARK TYPE

▲ **From below**
Dark birds have dark bodies contrasting with pale areas on underwing

IDENTIFICATION A race of the common buzzard, or perhaps best considered a separate species, the steppe buzzard is a small buzzard with rather short wings, less variable in coloration than the common buzzard. Typically it is grey-brown above and rich rusty-brown below with paler areas on the breast and underwing, a striking whiter patch inside the black wingtip, and conspicuous dark trailing edges to the wings (less so on juveniles). The tail is pale, flushed orange or orange-buff, and often looks translucent pale orange on a soaring bird. Most have a small pale area on the upperside of the primaries (common buzzards show at best a narrow whitish mark). A steppe buzzard soars with its wings raised in a V and is a typical buzzard in its general flight action. Its call is the same loud, squealing or mewing note.

HABITAT Varied terrain, with plentiful woodland and patchy clearings; migrates over more arid areas.

BEHAVIOUR Its behaviour, overall, is much the same as that of the buzzard, but it gathers in larger flocks on migration, travelling to eastern and southern Africa. Many cross the Bosphorus at Istanbul, quite late in September and October (where most are probably common/steppe buzzard intergrades). These impressive flocks go south across Suez, and even bigger numbers migrate through eastern Turkey. In its breeding areas it soars in typical wide, rising circles and perches freely on poles, bare branches, and posts.

From above ►
Adult (left) dark form
and juvenile (right),
redder form; small
pale area on
upper primaries,
reddish tail

Juvenile ▼
Pale, with dark wingtips,
darker body; tail almost
translucent, tending
towards rufous

Flight ▲
Like common buzzard, with slightly
stiff, clipped wingbeats but frequent
wide circling on raised wings

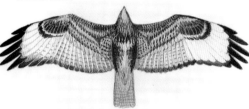

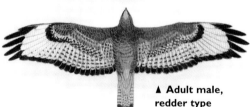

**▲ Adult male,
redder type**
Adult has bold dark
wingtips, wrist patches and
trailing edge; common type
has reddest body and tail

▼ Adult, greyer type
Similar pattern, but much greyer;
dark trailing edge and tail band
shows this to be an adult

Long-legged Buzzard
Buteo rufinus

50–61cm (20–24in)

DISTRIBUTION
Summer visitor to
C and E Balkans,
rare in Greece

▼ **Adult male**
Pale, with light cinnamon or sandy tinge
overall, especially on very pale, plain tail

▲ **Juvenile female**
Large, broad-winged, long-headed
buzzard with a plain sandy or rufous
tail, often looking much paler when
bleached or in strong sunlight

Dark form ▲
Some darker birds
much more solid brown
underneath, with dark
vent and rusty tail

▼ **Soaring**
Circles on raised wings like common
buzzard, but long wings and tail and
slightly bigger, more protruding head
give eagle-like proportions;
relaxed, flexible
wingbeats also
recall eagles

▼ Juveniles from below

Protruding head, very white primary patches, and pale bright tail common to all; dark wrist patches typical but may be less striking on juveniles

MALE

FEMALE

IDENTIFICATION A large, long-winged, eagle-like buzzard with an easy, graceful action recalling the rough-legged buzzard. It is bigger than the steppe buzzard, which often has similar coloration, and has markedly longer wings that give it a more impressive appearance. A long-legged buzzard glides with its inner wings raised like those of a rough-legged buzzard, and soars with its wings raised in a V and pressed forward, like the larger golden eagle. Its variable plumage has several distinct forms. Typically, a long-legged buzzard is rusty-brown or yellow-brown with a whitish head and a brown belly extending back to beneath the tail (this area is usually whitish on other buzzards); the rusty underwing has well-marked black wrist (or carpal) patches. The tail is typically pale, looking whitish at a distance with a rufous-buff or orange wash. Darker chestnut-brown and paler, almost white, forms are less frequent. Steppe buzzards are smaller, with shorter wings, and show less contrast between the pale head and dark belly. Usually silent.

HABITAT Mostly dry, open areas with crags, rocky gorges, scattered open woodland and large areas of short grassland; also seen over adjacent cultivated areas.

BEHAVIOUR This large, impressive buzzard uses the warm air of its favoured habitats to soar to great heights, but also sits motionless for very long periods on rocks, trees, or even flat ground. It searches for prey while flying in wide circles, or from perches.

Rough-legged Buzzard
Buteo lagopus

49-59cm (19–23in)

DISTRIBUTION
Breeds in
Scandinavia;
widespread but
scarce and irregular
farther south in
winter, rare in UK

Perched ▶
Sits motionless for long
periods; has 'frosted'
whitish head and
upperpart feather
edges, dark belly;
female has
longer wingtips
than smaller
male

FEMALE   MALE

IDENTIFICATION Slightly longer-winged than common buzzard, with more relaxed, fluid wingbeat; hovers more regularly. Typically 'frosted' whitish on head and body, with bold dark belly patch (rare on buzzard); paler underwing with black wrist and tip; white-based tail with broad black band. Pale long-legged buzzards similar but lack white tail with dark band; juvenile golden eagle much bigger, solidly dark on body. Loud call similar to buzzard's.

HABITAT Treeless tundra and high, barren plateaux; in winter occurs in lowland areas with extensive pastures, coastal marshes.

BEHAVIOUR Generally a shy bird, avoiding the vicinity of people where it can (unlike common buzzard). It perches on trees and posts in winter, but otherwise mainly on rocks or level ground. Soars easily to great heights on raised wings. It typically hunts by gliding around, with frequent pauses to hover expertly.

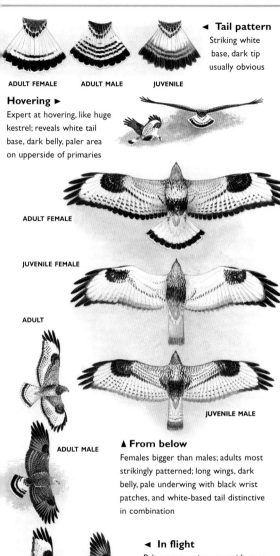

◄ Tail pattern
Striking white base, dark tip usually obvious

ADULT FEMALE   **ADULT MALE**   **JUVENILE**

Hovering ►
Expert at hovering, like huge kestrel; reveals white tail base, dark belly, paler area on upperside of primaries

ADULT FEMALE

JUVENILE FEMALE

ADULT

JUVENILE MALE

ADULT MALE

▲ From below
Females bigger than males; adults most strikingly patterned; long wings, dark belly, pale underwing with black wrist patches, and white-based tail distinctive in combination

◄ In flight
Pale area on wing upperside near tip (often on steppe buzzard, but smaller; rarely seen on common buzzard); action more flexible, less stiff than common buzzard

JUVENILES

Honey-buzzard
Pernis apivorus

52–59cm (20–23in)

DISTRIBUTION
Widespread but
local summer
migrant to Europe,
rare in UK

On ground ▼
Quite slender, or more
upright and squat

▲ Tail patterns
Male (left), female (centre),
and juvenile (right)

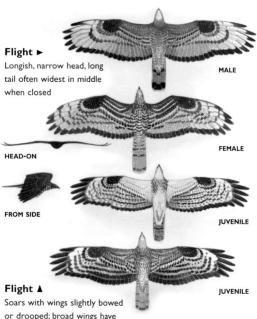

Flight ▶
Longish, narrow head, long
tail often widest in middle
when closed

MALE

FEMALE

HEAD-ON

FROM SIDE

JUVENILE

Flight ▲
Soars with wings slightly bowed
or drooped; broad wings have
S-shaped tailing edge

JUVENILE

IDENTIFICATION Not a true buzzard: it has a longer, narrower head and neck, a rather longer tail with a narrow base and long wings with an S-shaped trailing edge when soaring, or an angled leading edge and a straight trailing edge when gliding. Its wings may appear rather narrow, or broad and round. Importantly, it soars with its wings flat, slightly arched, or slightly drooped at the tip, not raised in a V. Very variable plumage, but two dark bars at base of tail and one at tip usually evident; handsome barred type has distinctive copious dark bars across body and beneath wings.

HABITAT Extensive woodland, with variable clearings or fragmented forest. Often in foothills of mountainous regions, with either mixed or predominantly coniferous forest.

BEHAVIOUR Usually a secretive bird, keeping well within the forest canopy except when displaying or moving to new feeding areas. Feeds by watching from a perch and following bees and wasps to nests, then digging out the nests over a period of days. Forms flocks on migration, using narrowest sea crossings in large numbers.

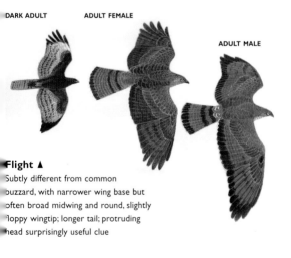

DARK ADULT **ADULT FEMALE** **ADULT MALE**

Flight ▲
Subtly different from common
buzzard, with narrower wing base but
often broad midwing and round, slightly
floppy wingtip; longer tail; protruding
head surprisingly useful clue

Variations ▶
Adult often grey-headed
with plain face and
yellow eye; juvenile
often whiter-headed,
with dark eye

JUVENILE **ADULT**

Osprey
Pandion haliaetus

52–60cm (21–24in)

DISTRIBUTION
Widespread summer migrant in N and NE, but local; also Mediterranean area, where a frequent migrant

IDENTIFICATION A big, eagle-like bird of prey, but with gull-like wing shape and relaxed flight, obvious at a distance. Dark upperside and pale underside distinctive; white below can look dull, or shine brightly in sun. Pale crown and black eyestripe usually easy to see. Kinked or angled wing with black wrist patch and dark central line below. Hovers and then dives for fish.

HABITAT Close to water on moors, in wooded river valleys, also on coasts, rocky islands. Often by lakes and reservoirs on migration.

BEHAVIOUR Spends much time perched on tall trees, rocks or other structures, but when feeding it flies steadily over water, pausing frequently to hover heavily and dive headlong for fish. Carries prey in feet back to a perch or nest. In spring, performs high, diving, undulating display flight with loud, whistling calls above the nesting area.

◄ From below
Obvious angle to wing in almost all situations, except when soaring on fully spread (but still bowed) wings

ADULT

JUVENILE

◄ Juvenile
Young bird has pale feather edges over whole upperside, often whitest on shoulder area; also has more rufous breastband

From beneath ►
Striking, long-winged bird,
with very white underside
and underwing; dark wrist
patch and barred hindwing;
often has dark band along
midwing area

▼ Hovering
Hovers well but heavily over
water before plunging for fish;
short-toed eagle also hovers and
has white body, but lacks dark
wing patches and white crown

JUVENILE

Adults ►
Adult plain dark chocolate
brown above; white head with
broad dark band diagnostic

Eagles

Most eagles have a regal look about them, their large eyes and big, hooked bills giving them a more majestic appearance than the vultures and buzzards. They also have an alert, intelligent air, as if ready for instant action, yet despite this many eagles spend most of their time sitting motionless on rocks or in trees.

Habitat
Wilderness birds

Eagles occupy all kinds of landscapes, from southern European woodlands and wide open, hot, sunny Mediterranean slopes to the great marshes of eastern Europe, the tundra of the far north and the mountains of the Alps and Pyrenees. Most species are scarcer and more localized than they should be, having suffered centuries of persecution as well as the effects of pesticide contamination. They are not generally closely associated with people.

The golden eagle is widespread but generally scarce. One of the truly 'regal' eagles with a superb flight action, it occupies a wide range of habitats but is chiefly a bird of wild, mountainous regions The imperial and Spanish imperial eagles are similar birds of more forested areas.

The booted eagle is a woodland bird, not much bigger than a buzzard, but Bonelli's eagle is a magnificent, powerful predator of ravines and mountainous regions. Another spectacular hunter is the short-toed eagle: one of the 'snake-eagles', it is a migrant from

Africa to warm Mediterranean regions, favouring bushy heathland with aromatic herbs and scattered trees. It hunts for snakes and lizards on open ground, so it often occurs over open slopes where the reptiles bask in the sun; intensive cultivation and afforestation have deprived it of many habitats where it once did well.

The biggest species, which looks much more vulturine in the air than the golden eagle, is the white-tailed eagle. Now very rare in most of Europe and absent from many old sites, it is doing well in Scandinavia and has been recently reintroduced to Scotland where it is beginning to thrive. White-tailed eagles live in mountainous areas with lakes, and on bleak, cold, wet coastal cliffs. They also occupy low-lying marshes, as do greater spotted eagles.

Extensive vistas

A golden eagle surveys a huge area of its feeding range from a prominent perch in forested foothills. It may also hunt over bleak, rocky slopes and peaks at higher altitude.

Feeding
Powerful hunters

All the eagles are opportunistic feeders and use a variety of techniques to secure prey. Golden eagles are among the most active and powerful. They catch hares, rabbits, and many other mammals, plus ptarmigan and other birds up to the size of geese. They are determined, strong hunters with huge feet, long powerful claws, and large hooked bills. The even heavier-billed white-tailed eagle also takes a lot of birds, but eats many fish – either caught alive or taken as they drift dead or dying on the surface. Both these big eagles also scavenge from the carcasses of sheep, deer, and other animals found dead on open moors, riversides, and coasts, especially in winter.

Short-toed eagles hover persistently, often at a great height, as they search for snakes which they kill by stamping with their stubby-toed but powerful feet. Bonelli's eagle is a fast-flying hunter of birds and mammals. The spotted eagles take mostly small to medium-sized mammals, and the booted eagle preys on a mixture of small mammals and birds.

Bonelli's eagle: a determined predator
Living in wild, rough countryside with forests and crags, Bonelli's eagle combines the size and power of a large eagle with the speed and agility of a goshawk.

Breeding
Long seasons

Eagles nest in trees or on crags. Golden eagle pairs may have two or three alternative sites, but tend to use a favoured nest year after year until it builds up to a massive structure of sticks, wool, and leafy branches. A few such nests in trees have been known to become so heavy that they have broken the supporting branches.

The usual clutch is of two eggs, but as one hatches a few days before the other, one chick is always larger and dominates the other. With golden eagles, the larger chick relentlessly bullies the smaller one, even if food is plentiful. Only occasionally will both survive to fly; the smaller chick is 'insurance' against the older one dying.

Unusually the short-toed eagle lays a single egg. This hatches after 45–47 days, and the young bird flies when 10 weeks old. These periods are similar to those of the golden eagle and imperial eagles. Breeding usually begins early and the full sequence – from courtship and nest refurbishment, through egg laying, incubation, and rearing young – takes many weeks.

Cliff nest
Several species of eagles, such as this Bonelli's eagle, make large nests of sticks and twigs on sheltered cliff ledges. They often contain sprays of fresh green foliage.

Booted Eagle
Hieraaetus pennatus

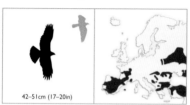

42–51cm (17–20in)

DISTRIBUTION
Summer visitor to
Iberia, Balearics,
S France, Balkans;
very rare elsewhere

PALE FORM

UPPERSIDE

DARK FORM

◄ Flight
Boldly marked; pale
form largely white
below; two forms look
similar above

RUFOUS TYPE

◄ Variation
Typical dark bird
(far left) dull
brown with paler
area behind bend
of wing; some (left)
more rufous with paler
flight feathers

◄ Pale adult
Fresh feathers very dark
brown, older ones fade
to brown or buff, giving
mottled effect typical
of most eagles

Variations ►
Dark and pale forms, and less
common intermediates, share
upright shape, slightly crested
head, and short, square tail

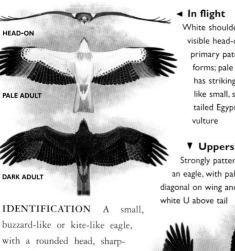

HEAD-ON

PALE ADULT

DARK ADULT

◀ **In flight**
White shoulder spots
visible head-on; pale
primary patch on all
forms; pale form
has striking pattern
like small, square-
tailed Egyptian
vulture

▼ **Upperside**
Strongly patterned for
an eagle, with pale
diagonal on wing and
white U above tail

JUVENILE

DARK ADULT

IDENTIFICATION A small, buzzard-like or kite-like eagle, with a rounded head, sharp-cornered tail and straight wings that are held flat or slightly drooped. A white spot at the base of each wing is often easy to see head-on but harder if the bird is circling overhead: if seen, it is diagnostic. Two basic forms: pale bird is whitish with dark flight feathers below; dark form is dark brown, recalling kite or marsh harrier. All have a paler patch behind bend of wing, translucent trailing edge to wing and tail, striking pale diagonals on upperwing, and pale U-shape on rump. Basic shape when perched is a little like a small, stocky Bonelli's eagle with a faintly crested head and densely-feathered legs; subtly different from buzzards and unlike longer-tailed kites. Gives a loud, liquid whistle in display.

HABITAT Hilly country and mountainous areas with woodland, thickets and open clearings.

BEHAVIOUR Booted eagles often fly in the open over woodland, but are frequently chased and mobbed mercilessly by crows and other birds of prey; sometimes this activity is a useful clue to their presence. They often soar at a considerable height and may dive for food in dramatic, high-speed stoops.

Bonelli's Eagle
Hieraaetus fasciatus

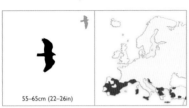

55–65cm (22–26in)

DISTRIBUTION
Very local and
mostly rare in
Mediterranean
regions; most
frequent in Spain

Adult female ▼
Dark grey-brown, white below with
streaks; tail closely barred grey;
long, densely feathered legs;
aggressive expression

IDENTIFICATION A big, long-winged, rather long-tailed eagle; in flight holds head up rather high, wings out straight and flat, giving a flat-backed, high-winged shape. Adult dark above, pale below with marked blackish band along the underwing, and a variable whitish patch on the back. Immature is distinctive bright rusty-brown with paler flight feathers below (smaller booted eagle has dark flight feathers, long-legged buzzard and much smaller steppe buzzard have dark wrist patches).

HABITAT Cliffs, gorges, high peaks, with variable amount of mixed or coniferous woodland. May be seen over high cliffs and peaks with barren, rocky slopes but more typically in ravines and valleys.

BEHAVIOUR A dramatic, dashing eagle when hunting, Bonelli's eagle will also sit on a rock perch for hours doing little or nothing and can be difficult to locate. It soars relatively little, and is seen more often in quite fast, direct flight with powerful, elastic wingbeats. It hunts rather like a goshawk, taking medium-sized birds and mammals.

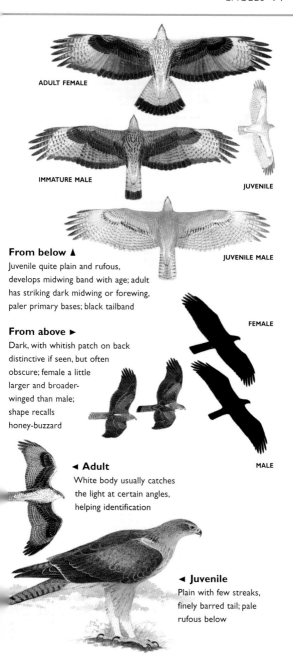

ADULT FEMALE

IMMATURE MALE

JUVENILE

JUVENILE MALE

From below ▲
Juvenile quite plain and rufous,
develops midwing band with age; adult
has striking dark midwing or forewing,
paler primary bases; black tailband

FEMALE

From above ►
Dark, with whitish patch on back
distinctive if seen, but often
obscure; female a little
larger and broader-
winged than male;
shape recalls
honey-buzzard

MALE

◄ **Adult**
White body usually catches
the light at certain angles,
helping identification

◄ **Juvenile**
Plain with few streaks,
finely barred tail; pale
rufous below

Short-toed Eagle
Circaetus gallicus

62–69cm (24–27in)

DISTRIBUTION
Widespread but local in summer in Mediterranean regions, S France, E Europe; very rare elsewhere

IDENTIFICATION A large, impressive eagle, pale brown above and whitish or silvery-white below; no dark wrist patches on the underwing, but variable narrow dark barring overall. Head may be dark, giving a hooded effect, with striking yellow eyes. The hood is least obvious on birds three or four years old; older males are paler than older females, which have the darkest hoods. Tail quite short but broad, banded darker. Soars with wings almost flat, tips widely spread and rounded; glides with wings slightly drooped and angled back; often hovers.

HABITAT Warm slopes and foothills with scattered woodland, extensive bushy heath and scrub.

BEHAVIOUR Often seen perched prominently on a high pylon or pole, or hovering (with rather 'wobbling' wing action rather than deep beats), or soaring high over a hillside before a dramatic plunge to take a snake or lizard. It frequently soars over woodland, its pale underside reflecting the green of the foliage beneath in bright sun. Displays (usually in pairs) with wings held very straight and round head protruding, making it look a particularly large bird.

▼ **Juvenile**
Neat, pale-edged upperpart feathers, bright buff wash around head and neck

▼ **Adult**
Narrow dark centres to feathers; variation in age of feathers gives patchy effect

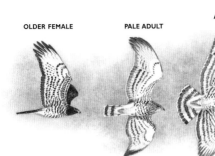

OLDER FEMALE   **PALE ADULT**   **ADULT**

ADULT

JUVENILE

▲ From below
Basically pale, but has narrow dark barring overall; often a darker hood; no dark wrist patches; broadly-barred tail

◄ From above
Mid-brown; adult patchy with wear, juvenile neatly marked with pale feather fringes; large, bulbous head distinctive

▼ Adult
Neat, sharp markings; extent and darkness of hood variable, sometimes almost absent on immatures, darker on older females

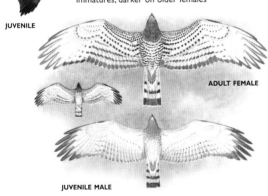

ADULT FEMALE

JUVENILE MALE

◄ Hovering
Hovers with tail fanned, wingtips angled back but broad, with 'wobbling' effect

White-tailed Eagle (Sea Eagle)
Haliaeetus albicilla

76–92cm (30–36in)

DISTRIBUTION
Coasts of Iceland, Scandinavia and Scotland; marshes of E Europe; almost everywhere rare; wanders in winter

From above ►
Dark overall; juvenile has darker hood, dull tail; adult has paler hood, often bleached to whitish, and pure white tail

JUVENILE

ADULT

On ground ▼
Heavier, less elegant than golden eagle, with deeper bill, bulkier body; heavy thighs but bare lower leg; short tail

ADULT

JUVENILE

▼ Juvenile
Pale face; dark spots above and strongly streaked below; tail feathers pale-centred, showing whitish streaks when fanned

JUVENILE

JUVENILE

IDENTIFICATION A huge, vulturine eagle with very broad, rounded, flat wings, a long, protruding head, and a short tail. Adults are pale brown with an almost white head and a pure white tail. Juveniles are darker, heavily streaked beneath, with a brown tail streaked with white, and gaining more white with age.

HABITAT Mountain lakes, extensive marshes and low-lying coasts, coastal cliffs and islands.

BEHAVIOUR White-tailed eagles spend much of their time doing very little, perched in a tree or on a ledge, but they can soar to great heights and display with dramatic aerobatics. They fly quite low when hunting, dropping onto their prey. They also feed on dead fish and mammals on the ground (sometimes with golden eagles, often with crows and ravens), or dive to the surface of the sea or a lake to snatch floating food such as fish or offal.

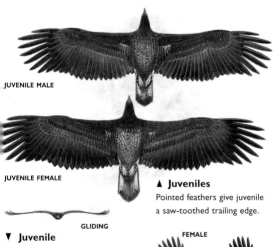

JUVENILE MALE

JUVENILE FEMALE

▲ Juveniles
Pointed feathers give juvenile a saw-toothed trailing edge.

GLIDING

▼ Juvenile
Big and dark; shape and attitude of wings separate from golden eagle

JUVENILE

FEMALE

MALE

Adults ▶
Female distinctly bigger and broader-winged than male, tail more pointed

Greater Spotted Eagle
Aquila clanga

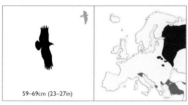

59–69cm (23–27in)

DISTRIBUTION
Rare in summer in
E Europe, migrant in
extreme SE Europe;
extremely rare
outside normal
range

◄ **Juvenile**
Several rows of white spots, lowest row
largest; long wingtips cloak tail at rest

◄ **Juvenile female**
Both spotted eagles have
long, slim legs and are agile
on the ground

IDENTIFICATION A large, brown eagle recalling golden and lesser spotted eagles; particularly broad, rounded wings. Most adults have greyer tail base, quite faint pale marks at base of the primaries. Wing coverts beneath tend to be darker than flight feathers (reverse of lesser spotted). Immatures have large white spots forming a band across the midwing above (three or four bands on juveniles), whiter U-shape above the tail, more distinct pale patch at base of primaries. Soars with wings flat, glides with wingtips drooped, unlike golden eagle but like lesser spotted. Loud, melodious, repetitive calls.

HABITAT Mostly extensive forest with lakes and marshes.

BEHAVIOUR Greater spotted (or spotted) eagles catch prey such as coots on the water, or take rodents (and some birds, reptiles, and amphibians) from the ground, either hunting on foot or dropping down from a perch or from the air. They also take many young birds from nests in colonies of gulls, rooks, and herons. Like other eagles, however, they spend much time perched and can be rather elusive.

ADULT

▲ Adult female
Very broad-winged eagle with
wide, fingered wingtips; round
head; shortish tail; small pale hook
or comma beyond bend of wing

JUVENILE

◄ Juvenile
Several rows of white
spots along upperwing,
white rump; same shape
as adult with large head,
short tail, wide wings;
adult plain brown above
with faint pale patch at
base of primaries, pale
buff U above tail

Flight ▼
Bowed or faintly drooped wings
immediately draw attention

ADULT

GLIDING

Sub-adult ▼
Dark, with paler flight feathers (palest,
least barred on male); pale comma
towards wingtip

Lesser Spotted Eagle
Aquila pomarina

55–65cm (22–26in)

DISTRIBUTION
Summer visitor to
E Europe, mostly
from Poland and
the Baltic states to
the Black Sea;
locally in Greece

ADULT MALE

JUVENILE FEMALE

▲ **From below**
Adult has forewing a little
paler than flight feathers,
unlike greater spotted;
thin double 'comma'
near wingtip; juvenile
paler, brighter brown
than greater spotted

ADULT MALE

GREATER SPOTTED

JUVENILE

▲ **Comparison**
Juvenile has fewer white spots than
great spotted; adult paler, especially
on forewing, often with distinct pale
patch at base of primaries; buff U
above tail, unlike any golden eagle

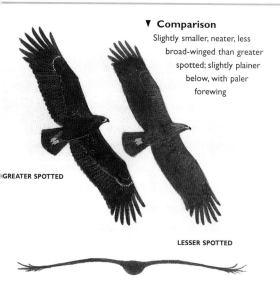

▼ Comparison
Slightly smaller, neater, less broad-winged than greater spotted; slightly plainer below, with paler forewing

GREATER SPOTTED

LESSER SPOTTED

IDENTIFICATION A medium-sized eagle, much smaller than golden eagle, slightly narrower-winged than the very similar greater spotted. Adults are warm brown, their wing coverts paler than the dark flight feathers, with fairly obvious paler patches at the base of the flight feathers and tail. Immatures have a white line across the upperwing and a pale patch on the inner primaries, variable whitish spotting on the underwing, and streaks on the body. Some are easy to confuse with some greater spotted eagles. Flies on flat or slightly drooped wings, with the wrist forming a distinct angle and the tips slightly lowered. Close reviews reveal a somewhat buzzard-like head and bill shape, less powerful than other *Aquila* eagles, including the greater spotted. Frequent short, musical calls.

HABITAT Large forests with marshy clearings and forest edges near lakes; drier woodland in Balkans.

BEHAVIOUR An African migrant, much commoner than the greater spotted eagle, which moves around the eastern end of the Mediterranean in large flocks in spring and autumn. It makes the shortest possible sea crossings, concentrating on the Bosphorus and moving through the Middle East. It hunts by soaring and dropping to the ground, or by watching from a high perch, or wandering on the ground on its rather long legs in search of small prey.

Golden Eagle
Aquila chrysaetos

80–93cm (32–37in)

IDENTIFICATION A very large but elegant eagle, smaller than griffon vulture but majestic and expert in the air. It shows a much longer head than vultures in flight. Adults are dark brown with paler blotching as feathers fade, and a creamy upper head and neck Juveniles are blacker with white on wings and tail. Soars with its wings up in a V, unlike imperial eagle, their trailing edges bulging in a shapely S-shape, but glides in fast, direct flight with wings flat their tips angled back. Much bigger, longer-winged than a buzzard.

HABITAT Mountains, bleak rocky peaks, high moors, forested foothills and valleys, locally on coastal cliffs.

BEHAVIOUR Spends long periods motionless on perch, but also soars for hours, often to a great height. Frequent deeply undulating display, ending in fast dive on bulging, swept back wings. Hunts by gliding quite low over open ground, chasing prey or diving in rapid stoop. Not likely to be seen on roadside poles or fence posts (which are commonly used by much smaller, commoner buzzard).

▼ Adult
New feathers very dark, old ones fade irregularly to cream or pale greyish

▲ Juvenile
Immaculate fresh plumage, feathers of similar age all equally dark brown; heavily feathered legs at all ages

▲ Juvenile
Dark, rich colours, often looking blackish, with variable but bold white wing patches; tail has wide white base, broad black band across tip; soars with wings pressed well forward

Adult ►
Looks plain at a distance, but close views reveal greyer tail with dark band, creamy area on upperwing

FEMALE

MALE

▲ Adult from below
Sexes same except for size and bulk; overall dark brown with greyer flight feathers

▼ Head-on
Circles on raised wings (left) but glides with wings flat or slightly drooped (right)

Juvenile ►
Upperside glossy dark brown with white tail base and white patch on upperwing, smaller than white area underneath; obvious pale crown

Imperial & Spanish Imperial Eagles

Aquila heliaca and A. adalberti

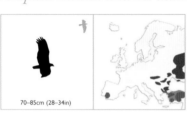

70–85cm (28–34in)

DISTRIBUTION
Spanish imperial rare resident in Iberia; imperial rare and local in Balkans

From below ▶
Very dark black-brown with paler grey tail base

SPANISH

IMPERIAL

▼ Head-on
Usually soars and glides on flat wings, sometimes raised

IMMATURE IMPERIAL

JUVENILE IMPERIAL

JUVENILE GOLDEN EAGLE

▲ Comparison
Golden eagle has broader wings, slightly longer tail, soars consistently on raised wings

◄ Tail feathers
Tail pattern develops from juvenile (far left) to nine years old (right).

IDENTIFICATION These are big eagles, recalling the golden eagle, but these two close relatives (previously treated as one species) usually soar on flat wings and glide with their wings drooped. Adults have a whitish patch on each side of the back, pale upper head and neck and a sometimes quite obvious pale grey tail with a broad dark tip. Adult Spanish birds also have a broad, striking white band on leading edge of inner wing. Immatures rusty brown below, eastern imperials paler but heavily streaked; from above, show bold black and cream bands on wing, whitish rump, black tail, and paler inner primary patch. Loud, barking calls given in flight over breeding area.

IMPERIAL

IMMATURE

HABITAT Low-lying areas with scattered woodland or parkland, extensive heaths and grassland.

BEHAVIOUR Perches freely in trees, resting inactive for long periods and difficult to locate. Flies quite low over open ground and woodland clearings, but also soars high up. Hunts by chasing birds flushed from the ground (often by its mate) and dropping to take prey such as rabbits, marmots and voles on the ground.

Juvenile ►
Dark wingtips and hindwing broken by pale area behind bend of wing.

Juvenile imperial ▼
Pale, sandy- to rufous-brown; broad dark and pale bands across wings; dark streaks underneath

Adult Spanish ▼
Pale shawl; white bands on forewing and scapulars very striking on oldest birds

Falcons

Falcons are often considered the most dramatic and dashing of all birds of prey, but although they include the high-speed peregrine and the massive gyr falcon, they also include small, insect-eating species that are much less powerful, such as the lesser kestrel and the red-footed falcon.

Habitat
Open sky hunters

Large falcons are fast-flying, dramatic birds and need plenty of space in which to hunt. Even the smaller species are superb in the air and can demonstrate their aerial prowess given the right conditions, such as in updraughts around quarries or sea cliffs. Gyr falcons and peregrines occupy remote cliffs on mountains and coasts, but peregrines now also nest on buildings in towns and cities, bridges and other structures, as well as in quarries.

Kestrels prefer farmland and mixed countryside, as well as heaths and moors. They are year-round residents, but several other falcons are summer migrants to Europe: lesser kestrels breed in hot, Mediterranean regions, red-footed falcons are eastern European birds of farmland and woods, and Eleonora's falcons are sea cliff specialists. Hobbies have recently increased in areas where flooded gravel pits offer new opportunities for feeding.

The lanner is largely a bird of semi-arid or desert regions, the saker a rarity of open steppe and marshland close to cliffs.

Most of these falcons can be seen almost anywhere as they wander in winter or migrate between their winter and summer ranges, crossing over all kinds of habitats, including cities. They range from common and widespread species like the kestrel, to rare and elusive birds like the gyr falcon, one of the most prized rarities over most of Europe.

Some are long-distance migrants, such as the lesser kestrel which spends the winter over the east African plains. Others move from upland to lowland areas or wander more randomly in winter, such as the peregrine and merlin.

Being at the top of a food chain caused great problems in the era of persistent pesticides in the 1960s, with massive declines in the numbers and range of some falcons. Better protection and the use of less dangerous chemicals have resulted in a widespread recovery, and some species have even spread to new areas – but others, especially the lesser kestrel, continue to decline.

Red-footed falcons: unusually social

Most falcons are solitary birds, but red-footed falcons can be seen in small groups in eastern Europe. Lesser kestrels are also social birds where they remain relatively common.

Feeding
Varied techniques

Some falcons, especially the bigger ones, are bird eaters: peregrines catch medium-sized birds in a dive from above, a level chase, or a delicate rolling 'catch' from beneath, while Eleonora's falcons chase small migrants over the sea around Mediterranean coasts. Merlins are the most persistent chasers, often following small birds for a minute or two in fast, twisting, low-level pursuits, but rarely diving from a height. Lesser kestrels hover in search of insects on the ground, while red-footed falcons and hobbies float gracefully over wetlands, catching flying insects in a series of rolls, stalls, and accelerating twists and turns. The kestrel is essentially a hunter of voles and mice, which it finds by hovering as if suspended on a string, or watching from a high perch such as a pole or wire.

Insect eater
The lesser kestrel is rather small and delicate: it can catch small voles and mice, but prefers large insects and small lizards which it catches on the ground, dropping from a perch or hover.

Breeding
Crags and ledges

Crag nester
Peregrines like broad ledges with a scatter of debris to cushion the bare rock, but make no nest. They can be encouraged to nest on buildings by providing special trays.

Falcons make no proper nests, but some species lay in the nests of other birds: merlins may use crows' nests in trees and bushes, and red-footed falcons nest colonially in rook's nests. Others, such as peregrines, gyr falcons, and Eleonora's falcons, prefer cliff ledges. Several favour cavities in trees or buildings: kestrels and lesser kestrels often nest on big buildings such as church towers. Some – especially kestrels and, in recent years, peregrines – will make use of artificial boxes or specially provided 'scrapes' on the ledges of high buildings, and often breed successfully if they have sufficient food.

Small species lay four or five eggs, larger species fewer; they hatch after three to four weeks. Parent falcons are often noisy and demonstrative around the nest. Once the young have flown, whole families may be seen flying and calling nearby for a few weeks; during this period the young birds are still fed by their parents as they hone their flying abilities and learn to hunt independently.

Red-footed Falcon
Falco vespertinus

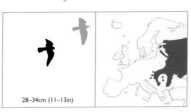

28–34cm (11–13in)

DISTRIBUTION
Summer migrant to
E Europe; rare but
regular late spring
and summer vagrant
in W Europe

Immature male ▶
One-year-old, frequently seen in
summer, like adult but with variable
pale collar, reddish breast patch,
barred wings and tail;
paler, less red legs

IDENTIFICATION A small, hobby-like falcon with a rounder, softer, slightly more kestrel-like shape; it often hovers in its breeding areas, less so on migration. The adult male is blue-grey with dark red thighs and vent, and red legs. The upperwing fades paler towards the tip. An immature male has a variable red vent, some reddish on the chest, chequered flight feathers below, and darker wingtips above. The female and juvenile are paler, barred grey above, buff below, with a buff or rufous cap, a prominent dark mask, and white cheeks; their legs are pale orange to reddish.

HABITAT Clumps of trees and woodland edge; marshes, dunes, edges of lakes; old or occupied rookeries.

BEHAVIOUR Often perches on a pole, pylon or overhead wire, or on a bare branch, dropping down to take prey rather like a shrike, or flying out to take insects in the air. Also patrols overhead like a hobby, but frequently lower down, taking insects in the air; more rarely chasing small birds. It hovers like a kestrel. A colonial breeder, with many pairs taking over the nests of rooks.

Adult female ►
Dark eye patch against pale head, white throat; distinctive combination of grey above, rufous-buff below; long wingtips beyond tail

Adult male ►
Deep blue-grey; red vent, legs, eye-ring and bill base; wingtips paler

Young male ►
Grey with rufous on chest and vent

◄ Juvenile
Broad white collar, dark mask, barred tail

◄ Immature female
Year-old grey on back, variable bars on tail and wing as new feathers appear; head fades paler (left)

In flight ▼
Longer tail, slightly blunter wings than hobby, shape nearer kestrel; softer wing action

JUVENILE

FEMALE

MALE

Hobby
Falco subbuteo

29–35cm (11–14in)

DISTRIBUTION
Widespread summer visitor in S, E, and C Europe, more local north to S Scandinavia

Adult ▶
Neat, crisply-marked; bold face pattern; rufous thighs and vent visible at close range

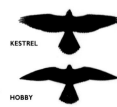

KESTREL

HOBBY

Flight shape ▲
Kestrel (top) broader, blunter, longer-tailed; hobby has sharper wings, like slim peregrine with narrower tail

▼ Juvenile
Pattern like adult but buff, less white, on pale areas

▲ Juvenile
Duller than adult, wears browner; paler crown and buff nape patch, but darker than young red-footed falcon, shorter-tailed than Eleonora's falcon

IDENTIFICATION A small, elegant, sharp-winged falcon. The adult looks very dark in the air, although the underside is largely white with close, dark streaks. A narrow black moustache and bold white neck patch are easy to see; the red vent shows well in good light but is often hard to see. A juvenile is similar but browner, and lacks the red vent and thighs: more like a young red-footed falcon but darker on the crown, less barred above and sharper-winged. Loud, high-pitched, quite musical *kew-kew-kew-kew* in summer, but generally a quiet bird at other times.

HABITAT Open heaths, farmland, vicinity of lakes, reservoirs, and pits, with scattered trees, copses, or adjacent woodland.

BEHAVIOUR Elusive in summer, but often easy to see feeding over wetlands or over fields where chafers are emerging at dusk. Takes insects in the air, using slow, patrolling flight with frequent changes of direction, stalls, turns, and marked acceleration to chase prey, including small birds. Also stoops onto birds at great speed.

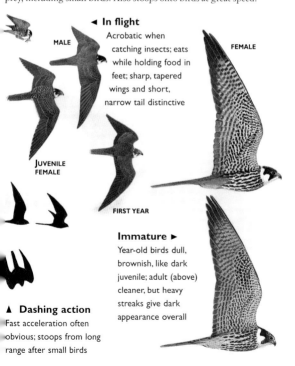

◀ In flight
Acrobatic when catching insects; eats while holding food in feet; sharp, tapered wings and short, narrow tail distinctive

MALE

FEMALE

JUVENILE FEMALE

FIRST YEAR

Immature ▶
Year-old birds dull, brownish, like dark juvenile; adult (above) cleaner, but heavy streaks give dark appearance overall

▲ Dashing action
Fast acceleration often obvious; stoops from long range after small birds

Lesser Kestrel
Falco naumanni

27–33cm (11–13in)

DISTRIBUTION
Widespread but rare, local, declining summer visitor; mostly Iberia, also extreme S France, Italy, Balkans

IDENTIFICATION Adult male richly coloured, like kestrel but plainer, with bluer head, plain back, grey patch on upperwing, whiter underwing with dark tip, and plainer, pink- or yellow-buff underside. Females and immatures hard to separate from kestrel and can be practically impossible unless accompanied by males. Flight a little quicker, slightly more whirring. Frequent squealing *vivivivi* and hoarse, chattering calls.

HABITAT Open landscapes, cultivated or rough grassland and heath with much bare earth; towns and villages with old buildings.

BEHAVIOUR More colonial than the kestrel, sometimes with scores of pairs together, but absent from Europe in winter. General behaviour is very like kestrel, hovering or hunting from a perch, or more infrequently catching insects in the air.

MALE   JUVENILE   FEMALE

▲ **Adult male**
Strong rufous and blue effect in good light; unspotted; bluish wing patch variable but diagnostic

▲ **Female and juvenile**
Like kestrel, with tendency for more distinct paler cheek patch; slender build, but hard to tell from the commoner species

Flight shape ▶
Sharp-winged in glide (above), blunter-tipped in soar (below); long, narrow tail with slight wedge shape

▲ Adult female
Underside like female kestrel, sometimes rather paler, and more finely-streaked on body, but no clear distinction

Female ▶
Like kestrel; barred rufous, greyer on rump, with markedly darker outer wing

Adult male ▲
Clear white underwing with darker tip obvious in good light, much less marked than any kestrel

▲ Heads
Female kestrel (top) darker than lesser (below)

Male ▶
Variable wing patch can be striking or more obscure; plain back

▲ Young male
Year-old has some marks above, some barring on outer tail: difficult to distinguish from kestrel

Kestrel
Falco tinnunculus

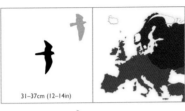

31–37cm (12–14in)

Beneath ▶
Both sexes have
silvery-white wings
with grey bars and
spots that flash pale
in bright light, but
look quite dark in
poor light

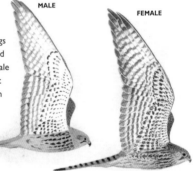

MALE

FEMALE

▲ Female
Underside like lesser kestrel
but only a problem in far
south of Europe

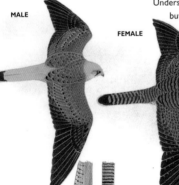

MALE

FEMALE

Male ▲
Grey, rufous, and black; immature
has bands on tail (right), replaced
by plain feathers (left)

◀ Female
Typical kestrel two-
tone wing and rufous
colour, unlike merlin;
long, barred tail

Perched views ►
Larger head, more upright than collared dove; rusty or ginger coloration distinctive at close range; wingtips fall short of long tail (compare with hobby)

MALE

FEMALE

IDENTIFICATION A small, slightly blunt-winged falcon, with a marked contrast between the dark outer and paler inner wing and back, shared only with the rare lesser kestrel. The male combines rusty brown, blue-grey, and brown-black, with distinct dark spots on its back. The female lacks grey and is closely barred rufous above. The lesser kestrel is closely similar. Hovering is a frequent clue to identity: in most of northern and western Europe it is the only small species to hover regularly. High, squealing *keee-keee-keee* calls have a nasal, strangled quality.

HABITAT All kinds of open ground from dunes and marshes to moors, with cliffs (both inland and coastal), trees, old buildings; also city buildings and parks. Less frequent in gardens than the sparrowhawk.

BEHAVIOUR Usually seen perched on a wire or pole with a rather upright or angled stance, or hovering – which it does more expertly and persistently than any other bird of prey – before dropping down to seize its prey. It also soars and displays great skill in the air, especially in strong winds or updraughts above cliffs, but it lacks the power of larger falcons such as the peregrine, or the 'menace' of a merlin. Kestrels often perch on ledges of buildings and readily use artificial nestboxes placed in barns or on poles.

▲ Flight shape
Wings tapered, angled in fast glide or dive; broader, blunter in soar

Eleonora's Falcon
Falco eleonorae

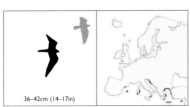

36–42cm (14–17in)

DISTRIBUTION
Scattered across the Mediterranean region on islands and some mainland coasts; a summer visitor

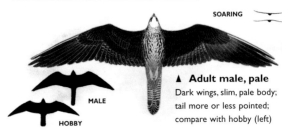

SOARING

▲ **Adult male, pale**
Dark wings, slim, pale body; tail more or less pointed; compare with hobby (left)

MALE

HOBBY

IDENTIFICATION A medium-sized, long- and sharp-winged falcon, more rakish and longer-tailed than a hobby or peregrine but sharing many of their features, Eleonora's falcon has several colour forms. Dark birds are all dark grey, often looking blackish against the sky (more so than a male red-footed falcon). The paler form is like a dark hobby, more extensively rusty below, with a black moustache and white cheek; the dark underwing coverts are helpful. Juveniles are more peregrine-like and the longer tail and wings may not always be evident: birds of prey can be surprisingly variable in their flight shapes depending on their behaviour and the angle of view. Nasal, harsh *kyeh-kyeh-kyeh* and sharper or whining notes near the nest.

HABITAT Breeds on coastal cliffs, hunts over coasts and open sea, and also over coastal marshes and rocky valleys leading inland.

BEHAVIOUR Small groups may be seen hunting insects over marshland, like large hobbies or red-footed falcons, or flying around colonies on cliffs, from which they fly out over the sea to intercept migrant songbirds. Sometimes several falcons will wait for approaching migrants just offshore. Active flight is quite slow with soft, shallow wingbeats, but when hunting it can accelerate dramatically and perform fast chases and long, rapid dives, combining the characteristics of the hobby and peregrine.

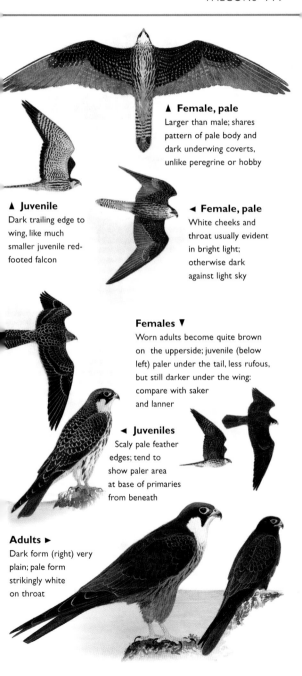

▲ Female, pale
Larger than male; shares
pattern of pale body and
dark underwing coverts,
unlike peregrine or hobby

▲ Juvenile
Dark trailing edge to
wing, like much
smaller juvenile red-
footed falcon

◄ Female, pale
White cheeks and
throat usually evident
in bright light;
otherwise dark
against light sky

Females ▼
Worn adults become quite brown
on the upperside; juvenile (below
left) paler under the tail, less rufous,
but still darker under the wing:
compare with saker
and lanner

◄ Juveniles
Scaly pale feather
edges; tend to
show paler area
at base of primaries
from beneath

Adults ►
Dark form (right) very
plain; pale form
strikingly white
on throat

Merlin
Falco columbarius

26–33cm (10–13in)

DISTRIBUTION
N Europe, locally in the UK; in winter moves south and into lowlands, wandering widely

Adult male ►
Smooth grey with dark feather shafts above, buff to orange-buff below; little pattern on face

In flight ▼
Short, tapered, sharp wingtip; male sparrowhawk with wings swept back may approach shape

MALE

FEMALE

Female ►
Dull mud-brown with faint cream and ginger marks above, streaked and barred below

▼ Barred tail
Female has bold cream bars on brown tail, unlike kestrel or peregrine

▲ Flight shapes
Typically fast, direct, dashing, low flight, neither gliding nor soaring very often; more compact than kestrel or peregrine

IDENTIFICATION A small, compact, fast-flying falcon, with broad-based but sharply-pointed wings and a rather short tail. Rarely soars or glides far; flight is typically low with rapid, deep wingbeats. Male is blue-grey above and bright buff below, with a dark tail band (unlike sometimes similar sparrowhawk); face pattern is weak. Female lacks rufous coloration and pale inner wing, dark outer wing contrast of kestrel; also lacks face pattern of larger peregrine; looks earth-brown with cream bands on the tail. Loud, variable *week-week-week* notes near nest, higher and sharper from the male.

HABITAT Open moorland or large clearings in scattered woodland in summer. In winter, on low-lying marshes, pasture, dunes.

BEHAVIOUR This is a dashing little falcon; when hunting it may fly with quick, short, outward flicks of the wings before engaging a small bird in a long, twisting, tiring chase. It often perches on a stone or hummock on the ground, or on a low post, watching for a chance to ambush and catch an unwary pipit or finch.

Juvenile ▲
Like female, but often more rufous and heavily marked underneath

Male ►
Tiny falcon with orange-buff underside; blue-grey back looks dark in most lights, but a colourful bird if seen well at close range

Peregrine
Falco peregrinus

38–45cm (15–18in)

DISTRIBUTION
Occurs widely but
sparsely in coastal
and upland regions,
wandering more
extensively in
winter

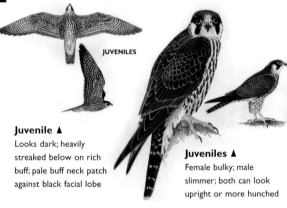

JUVENILES

Juvenile ▲
Looks dark; heavily
streaked below on rich
buff; pale buff neck patch
against black facial lobe

Juveniles ▲
Female bulky; male
slimmer; both can look
upright or more hunched

IDENTIFICATION A large falcon, female markedly bigger than
male, broad-shouldered and muscular, with a wider rump/tail base
than hobby or Eleonora's falcon; wings often curved in distinctive
anchor shape. Adults pale grey, paler on rump, white on breast and
pale below; blackish hood and face patch contrast with white neck.
Juvenile has similar pattern but browner-grey above, with broader
pale band on tail; buff below, heavily striped with black. Varied high,
wailing *kweeee* and *weep-weep* notes and deeper, hoarse, barking or
grating *kair-kair-kair-kair* around nest.

HABITAT Almost anywhere, from coastal cliffs to city buildings;
in winter often on saltmarshes, around reservoirs.

BEHAVIOUR A peregrine spends hours doing little, perched on a
ledge, post, or rock. In flight, it has a meaningful, menacing air;
direct flight is quick, with fast, deep, whippy wingbeats; it circles to
gain height before diving on its prey with a long, fast stoop.
Peregrines soar, often to great heights, on stiff wings.

Adult ►
Female very bulky, male slimmer; otherwise similar but male often whiter below, washed cleaner pink, less buff on chest, and bluer above

Juvenile ▼
May be more or less brown or brownish-grey, with paler tip to barred tail; bolder face pattern than merlin

Adult ►
Looks solid and muscular, especially broad across rump and tail; rump usually paler grey than back

Female ▲
Broad, bulky; straight wings may recall fulmar, even raven in side view; swept wings have anchor shape

Male ►
Lighter build than female, heavier than rather similar hobby

Gyr Falcon
Falco rusticolus

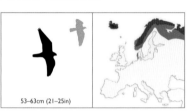

53–63cm (21–25in)

DISTRIBUTION
Breeds Iceland, N Scandinavia; moves a little south in winter but very rare far outside its breeding range

JUVENILE

Perched ▼
Juveniles have blue-grey legs and bill base, yellow on adult; also more streaked below

ADULT

JUVENILE

▲ Dark juvenile
Dark brown; head dark but much less of a blackish facial lobe than peregrine

▲ Head pattern
Even darkest birds lack elongated moustached effect but have dark cap and cheeks

Pale juvenile ▶
Lead-grey marks on white; blue of bill and legs separate from adult; paler than any peregrine

IDENTIFICATION Big, broad- and blunt-winged falcon with a long, broad tail. Typically lead-grey with only slight facial pattern. Young birds darker, browner, with more marked dark moustache recalling peregrine; heavily streaked. Vagrants to western Europe often whiter Greenland form. Typical flight is low, level, with slow, shallow wingbeats; soars on slightly raised wings and spread tail.

HABITAT Tundra and adjacent wild, barren areas; rocky coasts.

BEHAVIOUR Catches ptarmigan and willow grouse by surprise on or close to the ground. Although it appears heavy and relatively slow, it is a fast-flying bird, able to catch these grouse in a level chase. Sometimes chases other birds such as skuas or gulls for great distances, repeatedly forcing them to climb until they are exhausted.

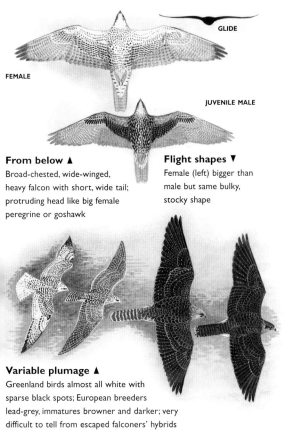

GLIDE

FEMALE

JUVENILE MALE

From below ▲
Broad-chested, wide-winged, heavy falcon with short, wide tail; protruding head like big female peregrine or goshawk

Flight shapes ▼
Female (left) bigger than male but same bulky, stocky shape

Variable plumage ▲
Greenland birds almost all white with sparse black spots; European breeders lead-grey, immatures browner and darker; very difficult to tell from escaped falconers' hybrids

Lanner
Falco biarmicus

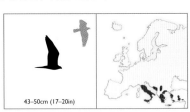

43–50cm (17–20in)

DISTRIBUTION
An extremely rare bird in Italy and the Balkans, much more common and widespread in Africa

IDENTIFICATION Looks longer-winged and longer-tailed than a peregrine, more like a very large kestrel in silhouette, with a more relaxed, flappy wing action. The adult is brownish-grey above (more bluish in Africa), pale buff below with dark spots on the flanks; the tail is narrowly barred, the head pale with a rusty cap, a narrow dark moustache, and a dark eyestripe. The saker is bulkier, browner, more streaked below, with a more spotted, less barred, tail and a weaker head pattern, but the two can be hard to tell apart in ordinary circumstances. Young lanners are more uniform above while young sakers show a strong contrast between the paler back and dark wingtips, recalling a kestrel. Loud, rasping *kr-eh kr-eh kr-eh*.

HABITAT Rocky, dry hillsides and cliffs; in Africa, more often in semi-desert areas.

BEHAVIOUR Pairs remain close to the nesting territory all year; the nest may be in a tree (based on an old crow's or similar nest) or on a cliff ledge. Lanners tend to wait for birds to come close, or flush them from the ground, rather than using a dramatic chase or stoop from a height. They can often be seen on telegraph poles or similar high perches with wide, open views.

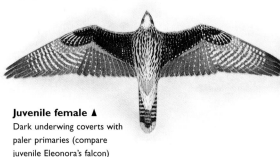

Juvenile female ▲
Dark underwing coverts with paler primaries (compare juvenile Eleonora's falcon)

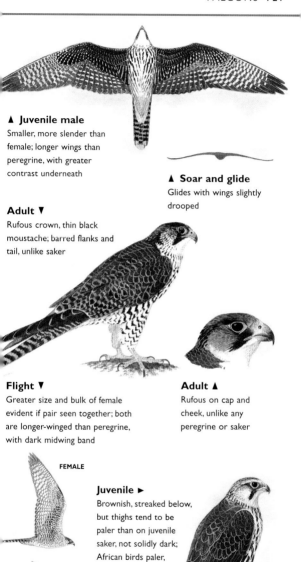

▲ Juvenile male
Smaller, more slender than
female; longer wings than
peregrine, with greater
contrast underneath

▲ Soar and glide
Glides with wings slightly
drooped

Adult ▼
Rufous crown, thin black
moustache; barred flanks and
tail, unlike saker

Flight ▼
Greater size and bulk of female
evident if pair seen together; both
are longer-winged than peregrine,
with dark midwing band

FEMALE

MALE

Adult ▲
Rufous on cap and
cheek, unlike any
peregrine or saker

Juvenile ►
Brownish, streaked below,
but thighs tend to be
paler than on juvenile
saker, not solidly dark;
African birds paler,
warmer brown

Saker
Falco cherrug

48–57cm (19–22in)

DISTRIBUTION
Extremely rare bird of E Europe, moving south in winter; more widespread in Asia

GLIDING

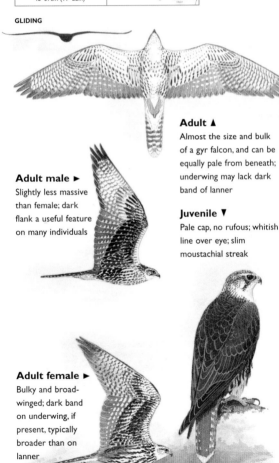

Adult ▲
Almost the size and bulk of a gyr falcon, and can be equally pale from beneath; underwing may lack dark band of lanner

Adult male ►
Slightly less massive than female; dark flank a useful feature on many individuals

Juvenile ▼
Pale cap, no rufous; whitish line over eye; slim moustachial streak

Adult female ►
Bulky and broad-winged; dark band on underwing, if present, typically broader than on lanner

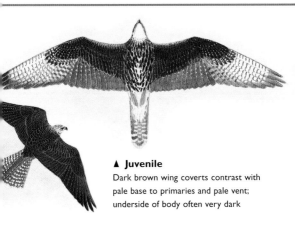

▲ Juvenile
Dark brown wing coverts contrast with
pale base to primaries and pale vent;
underside of body often very dark

IDENTIFICATION A very large, pale, brown falcon with wide, blunt-tipped wings but a slightly slimmer rear body and tail base than the gyr falcon. It can be hard to distinguish from the rather more lightly-built and narrower-winged lanner, but most have a more distinct two-tone upperwing, with the flight feathers darker than the coverts. It has a relatively weak head pattern, including a pale stripe over the eye, a narrow dark eyestripe and a slender moustache; it lacks the rufous of an adult lanner. Creamy beneath, streaked brown; the tail is brown with close pale buff spots on the outer feathers, rather than distinct bars, looking plain when closed. Juveniles can be much darker beneath with almost solid dark streaking, and dark wing coverts contrasting with paler flight feathers; the dark thigh patch is often a useful feature at all ages. They tend to be lighter, more tawny brown than young lanners. Can be confused with escaped falconers' hybrids. Calls are similar to a peregrine's, but more whining, less rough and harsh.

HABITAT Steppe grasslands with scattered clumps of trees and open forest; nests in trees, in old nests of crows and herons. Often found near coastal marshes in winter.

BEHAVIOUR A big, bird-eating falcon recalling the gyr falcon in its bulk and shape and general behaviour. It eats more mammals, however, and many fewer birds, usually flying down from a perch to catch its prey in a sudden flourish. It is mostly a fairly quiet and undemonstrative bird, but in spring performs dramatic high circling flights and fast dives over the nest site. This is a rare bird, threatened by continuing exploitation for Middle East falconry.

Owls

Owls are not related to daytime birds of prey, but perform a similar role at dawn or dusk, or during the night. While no animal can see in total darkness, owls have excellent vision in low light conditions. To supplement this good sight, they have sharp hearing that allows them to pinpoint sounds with great precision.

Habitat
From forest to tundra

Owls occupy a wide range of European habitats. Some are adaptable and wide-ranging, others more demanding in their requirements. Most are nocturnal, but several are also active by day: the little owl can be seen perched prominently in daytime, although it hunts mostly at dusk. Others, such as the tawny, scops, and Tengmalm's owls, are strictly nocturnal and generally very hard to find by day. Tawnies can be tracked down by finding splashes of droppings beneath regular perches, or following up noisy parties of 'mobbing' birds that have discovered an owl at its daytime roost.

Most owls are woodland birds, requiring trees for nesting and roosting in. At one extreme, Tengmalm's owl is a bird of deep, mature forest; by contrast tawny owls can manage well enough in

Tiniest owl
The pygmy owl is a bird of the forests and edges of clearings.
Round-headed and long-tailed, it is the smallest European owl.

town parks and suburban gardens with plenty of trees, although they are typically owls of lowland woods.

The barn owl hunts over open, rough grassland: it needs grass that is long enough to harbour plentiful prey, but short enough to make the prey easy to catch. As farmland has become less suitable in recent decades, barn owls have increasingly been squeezed into marginal habitats such as roadside verges, but these carry the risk of being hit by passing traffic.

Snowy owls are specialized for life on the Arctic tundra: of all European birds, they are most at risk from climate change, having no land farther north that they can move into. Eagle owls range through a great variety of habitats, from the pyramids of Egypt to forests and deep, rocky gorges, but they hunt in more open places, usually away from human disturbance.

Short-eared owls breed on open heather moors with tracts of rushes and grass, but also settle in fields and even temporary habitats such as overgrown building sites that provide food for a season or two. Closely similar long-eared owls are a little less nomadic, and prefer woodland edges, hunting at night over nearby heaths and moors. In winter, they roost communally in the tops of conifers, in dense hedgerows, or deep inside gloomy willow thickets.

The scops owl is a Mediterranean bird, living in open woodland, farmland with orchards, olive groves, and around small towns and villages, where there are cavities in trees and plentiful holes in old buildings, church towers, and under roof tiles. It is a night hunter, but can sometimes be seen beside street lights.

Several species live far to the north in old, undisturbed forests. The Ural, great grey, hawk, and pygmy owls are typical northern species, usually scarce and hard to find. The loss of mature forest with big trees is extremely damaging to them. This sensitivity to change emphasises the need for several kinds of feature within the preferred habitat of some species. While the short-eared owl is adaptable and opportunistic, even common species such as tawny owls have particular requirements, ideally including several large tree cavities within a territory, and barn owls require similar tree holes in which to rest up at times during the night, as well as for nesting in. Clearly the rarer birds of restricted range in the far north, or in isolated mountain regions, are the least adaptable and most at risk as ancient ecosystems are ever more subject to human interference.

Feeding
Dedicated predators

Owls catch prey such as small birds, voles, mice, and even earthworms, swallow it whole and then regurgitate the indigestible bits of fur, feather, bone, and beetle wing cases in 'owl pellets'. These gather under favoured perches or at roosting sites, and analysis of their contents tells much about owl food preferences.

Eagle owls are among the most ferocious predators, taking mammals up to the size of young roe deer (but more often rabbits or squirrels) and large birds. Hawk owls are bird-eaters, too, while great grey owls concentrate on voles and lemmings. Tawny owls catch rats around city streets at night, but also seize many birds that are roosting in trees, or even incubating their eggs. Barn owls, which hunt in flight and often hover, specialize in catching small mammals such as mice, voles, rats, and shrews.

Barn owl: a rodent specialist
Barn owls produce shiny, black pellets that are mainly composed of the remains of their favourite prey: small rodents.

Breeding
Varied strategies

Short-eared owl: opportunist breeder
Short-eared owls nest almost anywhere where food is abundant and where there is rough, undisturbed ground. They rear many chicks in good years but may suffer complete failures in between.

Most owls lay round, white eggs in cavities in trees or buildings, or in rock crevices. Short-eared owls, however, nest on the ground, as do snowy owls in the Arctic tundra. Eagle owls use cliff ledges, while little owls nest in piles of scree on coastal islands as well as in trees and roofs. Tawny owls readily use nest boxes in trees, while barn owls will occupy nest boxes in old buildings, in barns, or on poles placed in farmyards or close to the edges of woods.

Unlike most birds, owls start to incubate as soon as the first egg is laid. Accordingly the eggs hatch in sequence, one each day, and the first to hatch is several days old when the final chick appears. This usually ensures that at least the larger, stronger chicks survive periods of reduced food supply. In most years the smaller ones die, but in 'boom' years the whole brood may survive.

Barn Owl
Tyto alba

33–39cm (13–15in)

DISTRIBUTION
Widespread except in bleaker parts of N Scotland and mountain regions, absent from Iceland and Scandinavia

IDENTIFICATION A medium-sized owl, with a broad, heart-shaped or 'half apple' facial disc, a long 'snout' concealing a large, hooked bill, and black eyes. In western and southern Europe its upperparts are sandy-buff, variably spotted with grey and white in a 'salt and pepper' speckling, the face whitish and the whole underside white. Elsewhere it is darker, more spotted above and variably orange-buff around the eyes and on the underside. These 'dark breasted' birds sometimes wander outside their usual range. In flight, the wings are much plainer than a short-eared owl's, without any hint of a dark wrist patch; the dark eyes are a useful clue. Calls include a nasal *kit-it*, hissing sounds and a long, rasping screech.

HABITAT Typically a farmland owl, associated with extensive pastures or grassy patches, scattered trees, and farmsteads. Also occurs in plantations and woodland bordering moors and heaths, parkland with old buildings, quarries, dovecotes, and barns.

BEHAVIOUR Although typically nocturnal, barn owls also appear in daylight on summer evenings, when they are hunting to feed their young, and on winter afternoons when cold weather restricts the movement of their prey at night. They hunt by flying quite quickly, low down over open ground, often wavering, turning back or hovering, before a short head-first dive onto prey. At other times barn owls spend long periods in tree cavities or deep inside buildings, or in artificial nest boxes; heaps of shiny black pellets beneath their perches indicate their regular presence. Several large roosting cavities are necessary in a viable territory.

Hunting flight ▶
Large head, small body, broad-based wings held in a slight arch

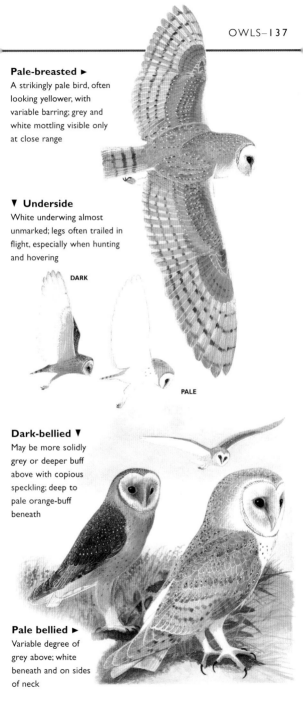

Pale-breasted ▶
A strikingly pale bird, often looking yellower, with variable barring; grey and white mottling visible only at close range

▼ Underside
White underwing almost unmarked; legs often trailed in flight, especially when hunting and hovering

DARK

PALE

Dark-bellied ▼
May be more solidly grey or deeper buff above with copious speckling; deep to pale orange-buff beneath

Pale bellied ▶
Variable degree of grey above; white beneath and on sides of neck

Hawk Owl
Surnia ulula

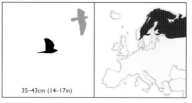

35–43cm (14–17in)

DISTRIBUTION
Locally through
N Scandinavia,
especially Finland,
east into Russia;
very rare farther
south in winter

FLYING UP TO PERCH

HEAD-ON

◄ **In flight**
Hawk-like impression except for deep
chest and rather large head; evenly
barred body and underwing

IDENTIFICATION A large-
headed, long-tailed, medium-sized
owl that resembles a hawk in flight. It
is dark above, white below with close dark
bars. The largely white face is outlined in black, creating a fierce
expression, with small, yellow eyes. Has a much broader head and
more thickset body than a sparrowhawk, but a longer tail than other
owls. Its flight is hawk-like with several flaps between glides and a
fast, upwards swoop to a perch. Rapid, trilling or bubbling song in
the darkest nights of early spring; alarm calls are falcon-like, fast
chatters, *ki-ki-kikikikikiki*.

HABITAT Forest and forest edge north to the tundra, with large
clearings, peaty bogs, plentiful broken or dead branches and stumps;
in mountain forest towards south of range.

BEHAVIOUR This striking owl is often active in reasonably good
light (in summer there is little or no real darkness in its northern
range). It can be seen flying across open spaces or over areas of forest,
or perched high on a tree top or on a dead branch giving a good
vantage point. It perches upright, scanning for prey or intruders,
which it attacks fearlessly and potentially dangerously, flying fast
and silently at the head: take care anywhere near a nest.

◄ From above
Dark, cooked-liver brown, with pale spots aligned along the shoulders; long tail unlike any other owl

Adult ▼
Bold face pattern very distinctive, as are long tail and white spots above closed wing

On perch ▲
Pale spots on back of head can seem like false 'eyes'; looks pale, frosty, about head and body with strong black band each side of face

Tawny Owl
Strix aluco

37–43cm (15–17in)

DISTRIBUTION
Most of Europe except Iceland, N Scandinavia, Ireland, mountain districts, and many islands

Perched upright ▶
Can be alert and quite slender, or relaxed and squat; some are greyer, others more rusty-brown; white spots on shoulder; black eyes in pale disc

Roosting ▶
Much rounder when asleep or dozing by day, head sunk into shoulders, feet hidden in the long body feathers

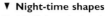

▼ Night-time shapes

Upright if alarmed; relaxed and rounder when feeding; looking down from perch for food

◄ In flight

Large, broad-winged, heavy, with very large, bulbous head; looks uniform brown above, whiter below, often very pale in headlights at night (compare barn owl)

◄ From below

Flights usually short, from tree to tree or down to ground and back again

IDENTIFICATION A large, robust, big-headed owl, with rich brown or grey-brown colours and line of pale spots along shoulder; wide, rounded facial disc and black eyes distinctive. Often a silhouette after dark, when heavy shape and round head without a hint of ear tufts help. Frequent loud, whining or nasal *ke-wick* calls and beautiful, slightly breathless, quavering hoot, especially at dusk.

HABITAT Woodland of all kinds, wooded gardens, and parks with dense trees such as evergreen oak, or thick creepers such as ivy.

BEHAVIOUR A strictly nocturnal owl, rarely seen (although occasionally hoots) by day, unless tracked down to a roosting perch in a tree, creeper or cavity; grey pellets are widely scattered, but 'whitewash' of droppings may be a useful clue. Hunts from a perch, or by searching likely places for birds' nests or roosting birds, even examining nestboxes and holes. Eats a wide variety of food, including many small mammals. Dangerously, silently aggressive at the nest.

Short-eared Owl
Asio flammeus

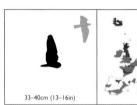

33–40cm (13–16in)

Perched adult ►
A pale, tawny-brown owl with
pearly-white spots and a broad,
white X-shape on the face
enclosing blackish eye sockets

IDENTIFICATION A large, long-winged, pale owl, white streaked with black below, with yellow eyes in black sockets in a whitish face. Mottled buff and brown body, dark wrist patches, broad, yellowish to orange-buff area inside the wingtip. Underwing whiter than on long-eared owl, with sharper dark wingtip; underbody paler; ear tufts very short and often invisible. Occasional nasal call; song in display flight is deep, booming, hollow *boo-boo-boo*.

HABITAT Moorland, heaths, open grassland and other rough ground with plentiful voles or mice.

BEHAVIOUR Hunts towards dusk or by day, flying low, harrier-like, with wavering glides, wings held in V; drops to the ground for prey, briefly chases small birds. Perches horizontally on ground or more upright on a stump, less often in a bush or tree.

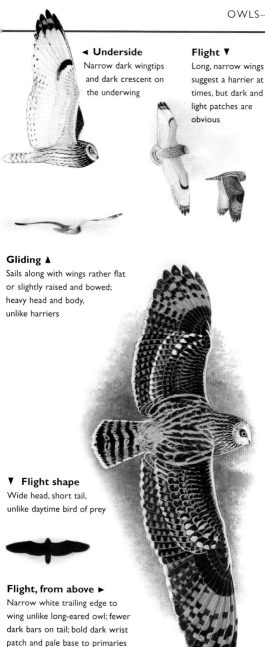

◄ Underside
Narrow dark wingtips and dark crescent on the underwing

Flight ▼
Long, narrow wings suggest a harrier at times, but dark and light patches are obvious

Gliding ▲
Sails along with wings rather flat or slightly raised and bowed; heavy head and body, unlike harriers

▼ Flight shape
Wide head, short tail, unlike daytime bird of prey

Flight, from above ►
Narrow white trailing edge to wing unlike long-eared owl; fewer dark bars on tail; bold dark wrist patch and pale base to primaries

Long-eared Owl
Asio otus

31–37cm (12–15in)

DISTRIBUTION
Most of Europe except far north; widespread in Ireland; local; northern birds move south in winter

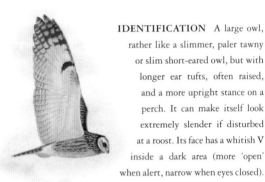

IDENTIFICATION A large owl, rather like a slimmer, paler tawny or slim short-eared owl, but with longer ear tufts, often raised, and a more upright stance on a perch. It can make itself look extremely slender if disturbed at a roost. Its face has a whitish V inside a dark area (more 'open' when alert, narrow when eyes closed).
Underside darker than a short-eared owl's, with heavy streaks on buff, contrasting with pale underwing in flight. Dark and light wing patches as short-eared, but pale areas often richer tawny-orange; more bars on wingtip and more closely-barred tail. Eyes are deeper orange. Song is a deep, moaning, cooing hoot or double note early in spring; young birds make a high, 'squeaky gate' note, almost disyllabic, *kee-i* or *kyeee*.

HABITAT Woodland edge of all kinds, copses, and various clumps of trees beside heaths, moors and other open ground.

BEHAVIOUR Nests in old nests of other birds in trees, especially crows' nests (or squirrel dreys) in clumps of conifers. It roosts in trees, such as tall pines or dense willow thickets, or in thick hedgerows, close to heaths, dunes, or rough grassland. Often roosts communally in winter. Regular roosts are easily disturbed unless they are approached with care. This is a strictly nocturnal species, much less likely to be seen hunting than a short-eared owl, but easily mistaken for one if seen in flight. It hunts over open areas adjacent to woodland, taking small mammals and birds.

▲ Gliding flight
Long wings slightly arched or bowed

Flight from above ►
Like short-eared but hindwing more uniformly dark, tail less clearly barred, more bars on wingtip

◄ Perched
Face pattern varies: may be 'squeezed' tight in narrow V or look rounder and more open when relaxed; ear tufts may be lowered

Scops Owl
Otus scops

19–21cm (8in)

DISTRIBUTION
Widespread
summer migrant in
Mediterranean
region, local further
north in C and
E Europe

▼ **Variation**
May be rather dark grey
with rusty patches, or
paler and browner overall

Perched ▲
Complex pattern of streaks and bars give
excellent camouflage against bark; half-
closed eyes may look dark

Head shape ▶
Tufts can be raised, spread
outwards, or laid back flat to
give rounder head shape

IDENTIFICATION A small, rather slender owl, but more rounded when relaxed. It has small, triangular ear tufts that may be raised prominently or flattened outwards to give a sharp-cornered head shape. Often seen in silhouette, when it is clearly slimmer than a little owl, and much smaller than the 'eared' owls. A good view reveals complex patterning resembling cork oak bark; the yellow colour of the eyes is rather hard to see. It is best located by its distinctive summer song: a penetrating, liquid whistle repeated 22–26 times per minute, with great regularity, *pew*; *pew*; *pew*; *pew*…

HABITAT Found in orchards, edges of woodland, woodland clearings, villages, parks and large wooded gardens, trees in quiet town squares, old buildings such as churches, and in old tiled roofs.

BEHAVIOUR A nocturnal owl, rarely seen by day, but sometimes giving good views if it perches close to a street light or perhaps a light in a woodland camp site. Its voice is by far the best clue to its whereabouts. By following up the first calls after dusk, it may be seen on a rooftop or church tower, or perched in the guttering of a town house, looking for insect prey. Once it flies to a new perch it usually disappears into the dark, and it may be frustratingly difficult to relocate. Favoured places are usually occupied year after year if the habitat remains undisturbed and food plentiful.

Flight from above ►
Long-winged, slimmer than little owl, with rusty areas on shoulders; no obvious dark or pale wing patches

◄ Underside
Looks rather uniform in typical brief views; slender form and long wings are distinctive

Pygmy Owl
Glaucidium passerinum

15–19cm (6–7in)

DISTRIBUTION
Widespread in Scandinavia and eastwards into Russia; more locally in C European mountain areas

IDENTIFICATION Not much bigger than a crossbill, and much smaller than little or Tengmalm's owls. It is round-headed but has a rather narrow barred tail, dark plumage with a barred chest and flanks, and a streaked white belly. The short, whitish brows over small yellow eyes give it a mildly questioning expression. The song is a simple fluty note, monotonously repeated every one or two seconds; also gives a series of short, rising, squeaky notes, especially in autumn, and a thin, blackbird-like *seeeeih*.

HABITAT Northern or mountain forest, especially silver fir or other conifers, but often mixed with deciduous trees in mountains. Also in cold, wet areas in the Alps, higher than other owls.

BEHAVIOUR Usually restricted to trees, making only short flights, although these are often fast and dashing. When chasing after a small bird it can be acrobatic, fast and persistent; in longer flights it has a deeply undulating or bounding woodpecker-like action. It often waves or flicks its tail, or sits with its tail cocked, giving the impression of a restless, unsettled bird.

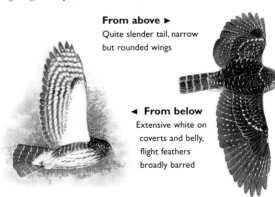

From above ►
Quite slender tail, narrow but rounded wings

◄ From below
Extensive white on coverts and belly, flight feathers broadly barred

◄ Comparison
Smaller than scops, much smaller than little owl

PYGMY   SCOPS   LITTLE

◄ Perched
Round head; short white brows; yellow of eyes visible at close range but face rather dark overall; underside neatly streaked

Rear view ►
Dark brown with small white spots; narrow, barred tail; round head on tear-drop shaped body

Alert and active ▼
Often leans forward and cocks tail on perch; looks around and searches the ground for potential prey

Little Owl
Athene noctua

23–27cm (9–11in)

DISTRIBUTION
Most of Europe
north to S Scotland,
Denmark, Baltic;
absent from most
of Scotland, Ireland,
mountain regions

▲ Small, round owl
Large, flattened head on
broad, rounded body;
large feet, short tail

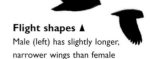

Flight shapes ▲
Male (left) has slightly longer,
narrower wings than female

◄ Perched
Large eyes and low,
pale brows give
aggressive look; bold
white spots on dark
brown upperside

Flight from above ►
Large, broad head, very short
tail; fairly obvious white
spots each side of back
and along midwing

◄ From below
No strong pattern, but
broadly barred flight
feathers

IDENTIFICATION A small, squat or upright owl, with a broad, flat or slightly rounded head, a fierce expression (whereas Tengmalm's looks 'surprised') with low, long, pale brows and pale yellow eyes encircled with black. Its body is largely dark liver-brown with pale spots above, pale with bars and streaks beneath. Its flight is deeply undulating and quite quick. Loud, ringing calls, *kyeeew* or a more hooting *gooo-eek*.

HABITAT Open farmland, parkland with old trees, rough grassland and heath, grassy areas with rocks or scree near coast and on islands, old barns and derelict buildings or ruins. Holes for nesting and roosting are essential.

BEHAVIOUR Although often abroad by day, the little owl hunts mainly at dusk, often on the ground where it catches worms and beetles. It is often seen on prominent perches, where it is mobbed by small birds; it may fly off with long, swooping bounds and a steep rise to another perch, or stare at an observer while bobbing, twisting and turning its head to get a 'fix' on the intruder.

Tengmalm's Owl
Aegolius funereus

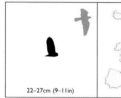

22–27cm (9–11in)

DISTRIBUTION
Scandinavia except
high mountains and
far north; also
mountain regions
of C Europe and
Balkans

IDENTIFICATION A small owl, with a large, bulbous head, either rounded or looking more rectangular, with 'bumps' above each eyebrow giving a hint of an eared shape at times. The facial disc is pale, surrounded by a dark ring; its wide-open, high, broad white brows over yellow eyes give a surprised or questioning appearance (whereas little owl is frowning; pygmy mildly curious). Large white spots on brown upperparts very like those of several other species. Much smaller than the sometimes similar-looking tawny owl (which also has black eyes and a duller facial disc). Pygmy owl has a more bounding flight and a smaller, rounder head, and tends to perch on more exposed perches, whereas Tengmalm's owl keeps within the canopy. Song is a short series of soft *po-po-po-po* notes, rapidly repeated; also a slightly nasal or muffled *chiak*.

▲ **Juvenile**
Very dark overall, with
bright yellow eyes

HABITAT Lowland pine and mixed forest in the north, often spruce, pine, or birch. Higher montane forest in central Europe, where black woodpecker holes provided nest sites.

BEHAVIOUR An agile woodland owl, capable of sharp turns and twists in flight in confined spaces when hunting, but usually seen perched or briefly in flight from tree to tree. Its flight action is rather even and flat, like a small tawny owl rather than the markedly bounding flight of other small owls. In hunts both within the dense forest or along clearings and forest edge, taking mostly voles, with fewer mice and small birds.

From below ►
Quite plain, dark body, paler underwing

From above ►
Like many owls, a row of white spots beside the back; fine spots on upperwing

Distinct expression ▼
A typically questioning or surprised look with high, pointed white brows

◄ Perched
Bright rusty-brown and white; yellow eyes in pale face

Ural Owl
Strix uralensis

50–59cm (20–23in)

DISTRIBUTION
Eastern Scandinavia
eastwards through
Russia; very local in
SE Europe.

PERCHED AND FLIGHT SHAPES

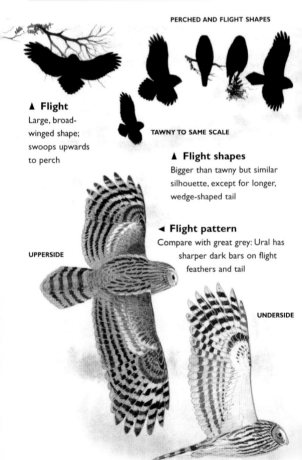

▲ **Flight**
Large, broad-
winged shape;
swoops upwards
to perch

TAWNY TO SAME SCALE

▲ **Flight shapes**
Bigger than tawny but similar
silhouette, except for longer,
wedge-shaped tail

◄ **Flight pattern**
Compare with great grey: Ural has
sharper dark bars on flight
feathers and tail

UPPERSIDE

UNDERSIDE

Perched ►
Small dark eyes set in round,
pale face with narrow dark
outline; greyish above,
broadly barred across
wings and long tail

Underside ▼
Front view reveals more
buff breast with fine
dark streaks

IDENTIFICATION Larger, slimmer
than tawny owl, with longer tail (recalling goshawk in flight). Pale
greyish-sandy with streaked underside; paler facial disc and small,
dark eyes give characteristic bland expression. In flight has pale area
towards wingtip, a little like short-eared owl but less contrasted, and
flight more buzzard-like. Deep, staccato *wo-ho; wo-ho, who-ho*.

HABITAT Northern and mountain woodland, with large
proportion of mature deciduous trees, often near clearings.

BEHAVIOUR Scarce, usually solitary, essentially nocturnal. Hard
to locate, but will attack people who come close to its nest. Hunts in
open glades or at woodland edge; in winter, often close to villages, or
around farms with plentiful rodents. Takes birds up to the size of
pigeons. Can catch rodents under 20–30cm (8–12in) of snow.

Great Grey Owl
Strix nebulosa

59–68cm (23–27in)

DISTRIBUTION
Rare and local in
NE Scandinavia,
eastwards across
N Russia

IDENTIFICATION A massive owl, with a huge, rounded head and a broad, concave facial disc that is remarkably compressed in a side view, like a satellite dish. It looks grey and pale, with a soft, complex pattern, broad buff patches on the open wings and rather small, yellow eyes. Longer-tailed than eagle owl; longer-winged, less barred than Ural owl. Song is a short sequence of deep, bittern-like, soft booming hoots; also gives various growling and hissing noises and a high, hoarse *chiep chiep chiep* in alarm.

HABITAT Dense forests of mature pine, with variable mixture of other conifers and deciduous trees, mostly in lowland areas.

BEHAVIOUR A fierce, diurnal owl, that sometimes attacks people close to the nest with silent dives. Flies with a steady, slow, rather heron-like action and perches upright in tall trees or on a high branches. It eats relatively small prey, mostly voles. It often takes its prey from beneath snow, diving down and digging deep. When hunting it usually glides down from a perch, but may hover and dive from the air, to disappear head first into the snow.

◄ Perched
Grey, with
complex pattern but
little contrast apart from
dark bars on wings

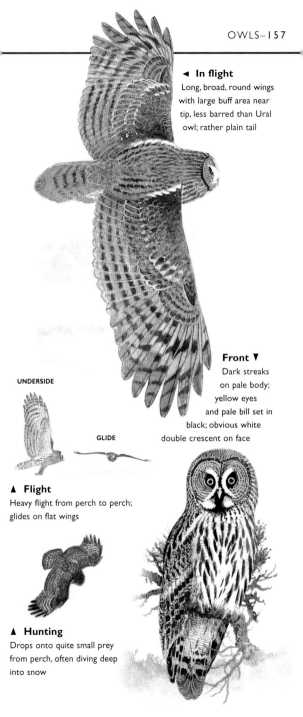

◄ In flight
Long, broad, round wings with large buff area near tip, less barred than Ural owl; rather plain tail

Front ▼
Dark streaks on pale body; yellow eyes and pale bill set in black; obvious white double crescent on face

UNDERSIDE

GLIDE

▲ Flight
Heavy flight from perch to perch; glides on flat wings

▲ Hunting
Drops onto quite small prey from perch, often diving deep into snow

Eagle Owl
Bubo bubo

59–73cm (23–29in)

DISTRIBUTION
Widespread but everywhere local in C and E Europe, rare in N and W Europe; resident

Flight pattern ▶
Big, heavy, wide-winged bird with plain brown appearance; narrow bars visible in good view

IDENTIFICATION A very large owl, buzzard-like in its bulk and heavy flight but with even broader wings. It is more or less plain brown from a distance, some being much blacker above, others more tawny-buff, especially below, with an even pattern of dark bars and streaks. The facial disc is poorly developed, but the ear tufts are long, mobile and pointed. It calls early in the year with deep, hollow *oo-uh* hoots; also much louder, sharp barking notes in alarm.

HABITAT Rocky mountainsides, ravines and cliffs with scattered mature coniferous trees, or more developed forest.

BEHAVIOUR An almost entirely nocturnal owl, which spends the day deep inside a tree cavity or small cave. It nests on a sheltered, secluded cliff ledge or inside a rock cavity of some kind. It is a fierce predator, able to kill medium-sized mammals and large birds, including other owls and birds of prey.

Alarm ▶
Long ear tufts raised
in alarm; orange eyes
open wide

Underside ▲
Pale underwing with dark tips,
fine bars; dark, streaked body
like giant long-eared owl

◀ Perched
Variable blackish
bars and mottles on
back and wings; often
rather rufous-tawny
around head
and neck

Snowy Owl
Nyctea scandiaca

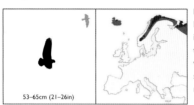

53–65cm (21–26in)

DISTRIBUTION
Rare, local, erratic
in mountains and
tundra of far north;
very rare vagrant
south of breeding
range

IDENTIFICATION An easy bird to identify, whiter than any
other owl (lacking any trace of barn owl's golden-tawny upperside);
much rounder-headed and broader-winged than white gyr falcon.
A very large, mostly white owl with variable barring (most on
immatures, then females, least on adult males). Yellow eyes look dark
at a distance. Flight distinctive: low, quite direct, with slow
downstroke and quicker upstroke.

HABITAT Open, treeless tundra, rocky ridges and scree slopes,
high, rocky plateaux above the tree line.

BEHAVIOUR This dramatic, charismatic northern owl varies in
numbers with its food supply: it has in the past
moved south, breeding in Shetland for a few years,
but faces a severe threat as its preferred
habitat is squeezed further north
by climate change. It is a
terrestrial bird, which
often perches on low rocks
or ridges with a good view.
It catches small to medium-
sized birds and mammals,
especially lemmings.

Juvenile ▲
Looks dull, flat grey with white face;
close bars revealed at close range

◄ Adult males
White with narrow
bars and wingtip
markings, gradually
reduced with age:
older birds pure white

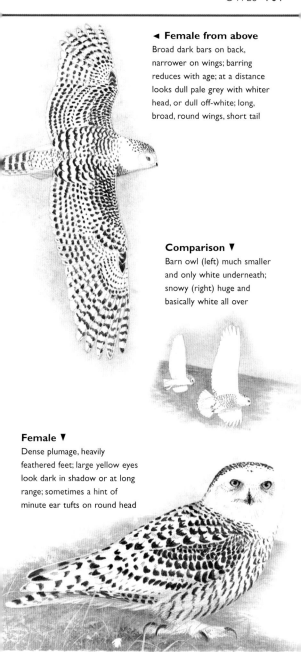

◄ Female from above
Broad dark bars on back, narrower on wings; barring reduces with age; at a distance looks dull pale grey with whiter head, or dull off-white; long, broad, round wings, short tail

Comparison ▼
Barn owl (left) much smaller and only white underneath; snowy (right) huge and basically white all over

Female ▼
Dense plumage, heavily feathered feet; large yellow eyes look dark in shadow or at long range; sometimes a hint of minute ear tufts on round head

Shrikes

Shrikes are not birds of prey, but songbirds that share some of their behavioural characteristics. They are bold, upright, alert birds, typically seen perched on high branches or overhead wires, but can be elusive. They often hold their tails at odd angles, or wave them, to help keep their balance as they watch for prey.

Habitat
Prominent perches

Shrikes like open places overlooked by bushes and trees on which they select prominent perches with a good view. They prefer rough ground and tough, thorny bushes such as old hawthorns, and are not found in areas that are too neat and tidy, or intensively cultivated. They can be fast and dashing, chasing small birds with great determination, but do not soar or glide like true birds of prey. Open ground with short grass or bare earth is essential, as they take a lot of small prey on the ground.

Red backed shrikes used to breed in extensive clumps of gorse beside open heaths in Britain, and were once widespread in ordinary hedgerows and low thickets near grassy areas, but they have been absent for many years except as scarce spring and autumn migrants. It may be a lack of food, especially large beetles and bees, rather than loss of habitat, that caused their disappearance. Migrants are usually found on the coast, in small bushes or buckthorn thickets. In Spain, breeding red-backed shrikes prefer small pastures and dense hedges in the cooler foothills, while woodchat shrikes occupy similar places at lower altitude, where it is usually warmer and drier. These striking little birds are commonly seen on roadside wires. They seem to require at least some small areas of bare sandy ground within the territory, probably on which to find large insect prey with ease.

Great grey shrikes prefer open moorland with scattered bushes. They breed in birch woodland with clearings, peaty bogs with scattered pines and beside clearings in northern pine forests. In winter they move south and west to milder places, but still have a liking for rough ground. In the south, southern grey shrikes and lesser grey shrikes favour slopes covered with typical Mediterranean scrub, olive and walnut orchards, thickets beside marshes and dunes, and similar places. Southern grey shrikes often occur in bushes on coastal dunes or at the edges of sandy beaches. Lesser greys are birds of warm lowland areas with long periods of sunshine, in strong contrast to the more northerly great grey shrike. Like other shrikes, it has quickly taken advantage of the opportunities for easy scanning of the ground for prey provided by ubiquitous overhead telephone wires.

Open country

Like other shrikes, the stocky, long-winged lesser grey shrike is never found in closed woodland. It prefers cultivated land, orchards, and other open areas with scattered trees and low thickets.

All shrikes are migrants: the red-backed, woodchat, and lesser grey move to Africa in winter, while the more northerly great grey shrike moves south within Europe to avoid extreme winter weather. They may return to favoured spots for several years, but are often nomadic birds that turn up for a day or two, or a few weeks, in quite unexpected places, never to return.

Feeding
Predatory songbirds

Shrikes watch for prey from good vantage points, such as bush tops, exposed branches of trees, poles, and overhead wires. They occasionally fly out to hover briefly over more open ground and scan it for food. Normally a shrike will drop from its perch or fly just a short distance to catch prey such as large beetles, small reptiles, voles, and mice. It takes its prey back to a perch, where it typically holds it under one foot and dismembers with its sharp, hooked bill, which has a small 'tooth' on the cutting edge to help kill and break up prey. Sometimes it impales insects, reptiles, or small rodents on thorns or even barbed wire, either to secure them while it eats them there and then, or to save them for later. Shrikes were once called 'butcherbirds' because of this gruesome habit.

Shrikes also catch small birds, usually after short chases, but sometimes taking them by surprise in bushes or hedges. They kill various species up to about their own size as the opportunity arises, but they are not specialist bird-hunters.

In most parts of Europe intensive cultivation and the use of pesticides has reduced the number of large insects, such as big beetles. Shrikes are soon eliminated from land that is planted with cereal crops or oilseed rape, or intensively grazed with livestock, and their future is insecure in many regions.

Vantage point
Perched on the top of a spindly bush, this woodchat shrike is alert to every movement and ready to swoop down on a beetle or lizard.

Breeding
Bush nesters

Bush nest
A female woodchat shrike visits the nest to feed a hungry brood. Both parents feed and care for the young, although for the first few days the female remains at the nest and the male brings all the food.

Shrikes are monogamous and territorial, never showing any inclination to nest or roost in groups. A pair can be very secretive when nesting, but the male usually sings in spring to proclaim its territory. In some species the male and female look almost alike, while in others, and especially the red-backed shrike, the difference between the sexes is very marked.

Their nests are quite neat cup-shaped constructions, made of small twigs, grasses, and other vegetation. The nest is built mainly by the female. Most nests are well hidden within bushes or small, dense trees, but some are in more exposed sites, even in woodpiles.

In northern Europe, great grey shrikes lay eggs in late May and June. Typically five eggs are incubated for 15–17 days, and the young fly when 15–18 days old. In southern Europe, smaller woodchat shrikes lay five or six eggs from early May onwards; they hatch after 14–15 days, and the young fly when 15–18 days old. Only very rarely is a second brood reared.

Lesser Grey Shrike
Lanius minor

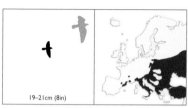

19–21cm (8in)

DISTRIBUTION
Local summer
migrant in S France,
more common
eastwards to
Balkans and around
Black Sea

Adults ▼

Pale grey above, white flushed pink
below; broad black forehead band
and eye patch; long, pointed wingtip
extends beyond tail base

MALE

JUVENILE

FIRST AUTUMN

Juvenile ▲

Looks duller, washed brownish;
faint bars above; by late autumn
grey above, but still lacks black
forehead of adult

IDENTIFICATION The adult is pale grey, black, and white, with a strong pinkish flush beneath, recalling the great grey and southern grey shrikes. The broad black mask extends characteristically over the forehead (sometimes mottled with grey on the female), quite unlike a great grey shrike; the bill is distinctively thick and stubby. A useful feature in a close view is the rather long, slender wingtip, extending further down the tail than on a great grey shrike. Juveniles share the same structural features, including the thick bill and long wing. They are barred above, but not beneath, and the forehead is grey, inviting confusion with the great grey shrike, but note the broad white wing patch and squarer tail. Has several harsh, chattering notes such as *tche-tche-tche* and a varied musical and rasping song with distinctive screeching notes; this is often given in a bouncy, hovering song flight.

HABITAT Open countryside with scattered trees, farmland, heaths, scrubby thickets with clearings, and orchards.

BEHAVIOUR A typical shrike, often seen perched on a wire or on a prominent twig on the outside of a tree, from which it watches for potential prey. It catches large insects, especially beetles, small reptiles, and small rodents on the ground, and chases small birds in flight.

Flight from below ▲
Tapered, pointed wingtip; very broad white band across flight feathers; pink underside may be obvious in bright light

From above ▲
Striking pattern with bold white patch on long, black wing, broad white sides to black-centred tail, mid-grey back

Great Grey Shrike
Lanius excubitor

22–26cm (9–10in)

DISTRIBUTION
Great grey breeds in N Europe, moves further south and west in winter; southern grey mostly in S France and Iberia

IDENTIFICATION A large, round-tailed shrike with slimmer bill and shorter wingtip than lesser grey; black eye patch does not reach forehead, but is narrowly edged with white above. Female faintly barred below; juvenile barred on breast, but otherwise plain, with weaker eye patch. Several races/species: southern grey of Iberia slightly darker above and obviously darker, dull buff-pink below; steppe grey of Asia very pale. Infrequent harsh, chacking calls.

EASTERN FORM

HABITAT Northern birds breed in upland or far northern birch forest, and clearings in pine woods. In winter occurs in boggy clearings, on heaths, and on farmland with rough grass. Southern grey in open, dry, warm, bushy countryside.

BEHAVIOUR Typically on exposed branch, post, or wire, but elusive at times. Looks for prey on the ground and chases small birds; often swings tail for balance. A bold, aggressive bird. Flies with swooping undulations.

◄ **Steppe grey shrike**
Rare visitor from Asia: huge white wing patch, weak mask, pale around pale-based bill, long wingtip

Steppe grey shrike ▲
May show eight exposed primary tips on long, drooped wingtip

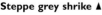

Southern grey ▶
Juvenile faintly barred; wingtip just short of upper tail coverts (longer on lesser grey)

Southern grey ▼
Southern birds dark, flushed deep buff-pink below; wide, short white wing patch (may taper inwards on great grey)

Southern grey ▲
Dark, like lesser grey; even darker beneath, but no black on forehead at any stage; longer tail

UNDERWING, SOUTHERN

ADULT SOUTHERN GREY

Great grey ▼
Northern birds pale; black mask broadens behind eye, edged white on top; white shoulder patch above dark wing with short tip; juvenile barred below, not above like lesser grey

ADULTS

ADULT GREAT GREY

JUVENILE

Woodchat Shrike
Lanius senator

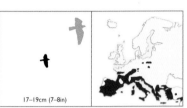

17–19cm (7–8in)

DISTRIBUTION
Summer migrant in
Mediterranean area,
locally north to
C Europe; scarce
spring migrant
further north

Adult male ►
Beautiful, neat shrike with
distinctive red-brown cap and
hindneck, black mask; broad
white shoulder patch

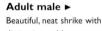

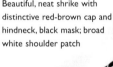

Male, Balearics ►
Breeding birds here have
all-dark wing, but typically
white on shoulders, rump,
and sides of tail

Adult female ▼
Variably greyish or mottled
face mask, duller cap

◄ Juvenile
Barred cap, scaly
pattern on whitish
shoulder, rufous
wing patch

FIRST WINTER

Female ►
Often less intense black
than male, with broad,
pale feather edges on
wings and less neat
facial markings

Underside ►
White coverts,
greyer flight feathers
with paler band
across base

Juvenile ►
Brownish, with whiter area
each side of back; pale
rump, buff wing patch

IDENTIFICATION A striking shrike with a
bold pattern. Adult is black and white, with a bright
chestnut-red cap; the female has a paler cap and less neat
black facial band. Shows a broad white shoulder patch, like a great
spotted woodpecker. The juvenile is pale, brownish, with a cold
greyish rump and shoulder area with darker, crescentic bars. Birds
breeding in the Balearics (race *badius*) lack the white wing patch,
while those in Turkey have a broader white band. Gives occasional
short, harsh notes and a loud, unmusical, squeaky and rattling song,
often with good mimicry of other species.

HABITAT Farmland with hedges, orchards, scattered trees, river
valleys with plantations, marshy spots, reeds, and thickets; very often
on overhead wires. Usually needs bare, sandy ground, whereas red-
backed shrike occurs in greener, grassier places.

BEHAVIOUR A bold hunter, the woodchat shrike often perches
openly on a wire or a high pole, but also frequently lower down and
much less conspicuously in a bush or hedgerow. It takes small voles
and large insects, and often catches small birds in a short, surprise
pounce or after a brief chase.

Red-backed Shrike
Lanius collurio

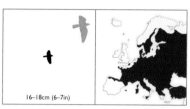

16–18cm (6–7in)

DISTRIBUTION
Widespread in
summer from
N Spain north to
S Scandinavia, and
to east; scarce
migrant in NW
Europe

Juvenile ►
Rather rufous, with dark
crescentic barring
above and faint or
more obvious bars
below; rufous tail

IDENTIFICATION This
is a small, smart shrike with a
longish tail and stout bill. Male
is rich brown above, pink below,
with a bold black band on a blue-grey
head; tail is black and white. Female is less striking, but rich, tawny
or rusty brown above, barred greyish on dull grey-buff below, with
an indication of a dark eye patch and greyer nape. Juveniles barred
above; may be brighter, rustier overall, or rather grey, without
woodchat shrike's pale shoulder patch. Short harsh or clicking calls.

HABITAT Heath edges with thorn bushes, gorse, rough thickets;
pastures with old, rambling hedges, wild rose, and other thorny
shrubs, often on higher foothills of southern mountain ranges.

BEHAVIOUR Often an inconspicuous, almost skulking bird, but
also frequently easy to see perched on a wire, pole, or bush top.
Catches its prey on the ground and impales large insects, occasionally
voles and small birds, on thorns or sometimes barbed wire.

◄ Adult female
Thrush-like, with protruding
head, long tail; generally
rusty-brown with darker
wings, plain tail; some have
greyer head (below)

Adult male ►
Immaculate pink, blue-grey,
red-brown, black, and
white in striking pattern;
bold face mask; black
and white tail

FEMALE

MALE

◄ Adult male
Blue-grey head contrasts
with brown back; black and
white tail; upright stance

Male ▼
Plain, dark wings without white,
but wide white sides to black-
centred tail

Index